MEDIAEVAL SOURCES IN TRANSLATION

12

THE BOOK OF THE COVENANT

OF

JOSEPH KIMḤI

Translated by

Frank TALMAGE
University of Toronto

THE PONTIFICAL INSTITUTE OF MEDIAEVAL STUDIES
Toronto, Canada
1972

Library Cataloguing Data

Kimḥi, Joseph, 1105?–1170?

The book of the covenant.

(Mediaeval sources in translation ISSN 0316–0874 ; 12)
Translation of Sefer ha-berit.
Bibliography: p. [84]
ISBN 0–88844–261–0

1. Christianity — Controversial literature. 2. Judaism — Apologetic works. I. Talmage, Frank Ephraim. II. Pontifical Institute of Mediaeval Studies. III. Kimḥi, Joseph, 1105?–1170? IV. Title V. Series.

BM590.K5613 296.3

Pontifical Institute of Mediaeval Studies
59 Queen's Park Crescent East
Toronto, Ontario, Canada M5S 2C4

PRINTED BY UNIVERSA, WETTEREN, BELGIUM

In memory of my friend

Gunter Sieburth

Psalms 25:13

TABLE OF CONTENTS

INTRODUCTION

Of the personal life of Joseph Kimḥi (1105?-1170?) very little is known outside of the fact that he fled Spain in the wake of the Almohade persecutions of 1148 (as did the family of the more famous Moses Maimonides) and that he settled in Narbonne. In Provence, he functioned as teacher,[1] translator, grammarian, and biblical exegete. Kimḥi was one of the pioneers in the translating of philosophical literature written in Arabic and rendered the ethical treatise, *Duties of the Heart (Ḥovot ha-Levavot)*, of Baḥya ibn Paquda (12th c.?) into Hebrew. He also produced a Hebrew version of Solomon ibn Gabirol's

*I wish to express my gratitude to Professor Judah Rosenthal of Jerusalem and Rabbi David S. Shapiro of Milwaukee for allowing me to draw on their vast erudition. Professor Hayyim Hillel Ben Sasson of Jerusalem made many important observations for which I render this single but sincere acknowledgement.

The following abbreviations are employed in the footnotes: *AJ* – A. Lukyn Williams, *Adversus Judaeos* (Cambridge, 1935); *JbR* – Jacob ben Reuben, *Milḥamot ha-Shem* (ed. J. Rosenthal, Jerusalem, 1963); *MGWJ* – *Monatsschrift für Geschichte und Wissenschaft des Judentums; MḤ* – *Milḥemet Ḥovah* (Constantinople, 1710); *Nestor* – *Sefer Nestor ha-Komer* (ed. A. Berliner, Altona, 1875); *SB* – *Sefer ha-Berit (Book of the Covenant)*.

[1] Among his students are numbered his son Moses, Menaḥem ben Simeon of Posquières, Solomon ben Isaac ha-Nesiah, and Joseph ibn Zabara. On Kimḥi himself, the basic study remains that of A. Geiger in *Oẓar Neḥmad* I (1856), 97ff.; II (1857), 98f.; III (1858), 114f. See the bibliography in *Encyclopedia Judaica* (1934), IX, 1244. On the name Kimḥi, see M. Steinschneider in *MGWJ* XXXV (1885), 528; *Allgemeine Zeitung des Judentums,* 1864, nr. 5, 89; A. Neubauer, *Journal Asiatique*, 5th ser., XX (1862), 251f. The Kimḥi family also bore the French surname Petit. See H. Gross, *Gallia Judaica* (Paris, 1897), p. 385.

[2] A fragment of Kimḥi's translation was printed in the Benjacob edition of Ibn Tibbon's translation (Leipzig, 1846) and reprinted in the Zifroni ed. (Jerusalem, 1938).

(1021-70) *Choice of Pearls*, a collection of gnomic sayings, under the title *Sheqel ha-Qodesh*.[3] In the field of grammar, Kimḥi composed the *Book of Remembrance (Sefer Zikkaron)*,[4] a systematic grammar in which he made a number of innovations in the presentation of the vowel system and in the theory of the verb which were widely accepted until modern times. This was followed by the *Open Book (Sefer ha-Galui*[5]*)* consisting of two parts: a critique of Jacob Tam's (1100-1171) *Decisions (Hakhra'ot)* on the *Compendium (Maḥberet)* of Menaḥem ibn Saruq (910-970) and a compilation of Kimḥi's own critical remarks on points in the *Maḥberet* left untouched by Tam.[6] As exegete, Kimḥi composed commentaries on the Pentateuch,[7] Proverbs,[8] Job,[9] and the Song of Songs.[10] In addition, a *Book of Acquisition (Sefer ha-Miqnah)*[11] on the Prophets is no longer extant. Finally, because of Kimḥi's theological and exegetical interests, he was involved too in disputational activities with Christians and composed the *Book of the Covenant (Sefer ha-Berit)* presented here in English

[3] The *Sheqel ha-Qodesh* is extant in two recensions. See A. Marx, "Gabirol's Authorship of the *Choice of Pearls* and the two Versions of J. Kimḥi's *Shekel ha-Kodesh*", *HUCA* IV (1927), 438-448.

[4] The name is taken from Mal. 3:15. The *Sefer Zikkaron* was published by W. Bacher, Berlin, 1887.

[5] The name is taken from Jer. 32:14. The *Sefer ha-Galui* was published by H. W. Mathews, Berlin, 1887.

[6] See H. Hirschfeld, *Literary History of Hebrew Grammarians and Lexicographers* (London, 1926), pp. 24ff., 66. On Kimḥi as a grammarian, see Hirschfeld, *Lit. Hist.*, pp. 78ff.; S. Eppenstein, "Studien über Joseph Kimchi", *MGWJ* XL (1896), 173ff.; XLI (1897), 83ff.

[7] Citations from this were published under the name *Sefer ha-Torah*, ed. H. Gad, Johannesburg, 1952.

[8] Entitled *Sefer Ḥuqqah* by the editor, B. Dubrowo, Breslau, 1861.

[9] Partly published by Schwarz in *Tiqwat 'Enosh*, Berlin, 1868.

[10] In ms.

[11] The name is taken from Jer. 32:11 et seq. Much of Kimḥi's exegesis has been preserved in the commentaries of his sons, Moses and David, Menaḥem ben Simeon, and Jacob ben Asher.

translation.[12] Our author was the father of two distinguished grammarians and exegetes, Moses Kimḥi (d. ca. 1190)[13] and David Kimḥi (1160?-1235?), one of the pillars of medieval Jewish scholarship.[14]

Upon arrival in Narbonne, Kimḥi found a community already well established and "widely respected throughout Jewish Europe for its wideranging rabbinic scholarship and deep-rooted piety, whose sages were constantly beseeched for scholarly advice and learned guidance".[15] It was at this time that Provence was making its "literary debut ... accomplished with great intensity and originality, and the twelfth century ... is marked by dynamic study of Talmudic literature and midrash and innovation in halakic ideas, methods, and literary genres".[16] Those scholars, such as Kimḥi and his compatriot Judah ibn Tibbon (1120-1190), who arrived in Provence from Muslim Spain acknowledged this tradition of learning but found it wanting in certain respects. Ibn Tibbon remarks:

> Also in the lands of the Christians there was a remnant for our people. From the earliest days [of their settlement] there were among them scholars proficient in the knowledge of Torah and Talmud, but they did not occupy themselves with other sciences because their Torah-study was their [sole] profession and because books about other sciences were not available in their regions.[17]

[12] See below, p. 16.

[13] For bibliography, see *Enc. Jud.*, IX, 1246.

[14] For bibliography, see Enc. Jud., IX, 1239 and F. Talmage, "David Kimḥi as Polemicist," *Hebrew Union College Annual* XXVIII (1967), 213-235; "David Kimḥi and the Rationalist Tradition", *HUCA* XXXIX (1968), 179-218.

[15] I. Twersky, "Aspects of the Social and Cultural History of Provençal Jewry", *Journal of World History*, XI (1968), 191. For a contemporary description of Kimḥi's Provence, see Benjamin ben Jonah of Tudela, *The Itinerary of Benjamin of Tudela*, ed. Marcus N. Adler (1907).

[16] *Ibid.*

[17] Int. to Baḥya's *Duties of the Heart*, ed. A. Zifroni (Jerusalem, 1938), cited from Twersky, *ibid.*, p. 195.

It was the task of Kimḥi in his way and of the translator Ibn Tibbon in his to introduce extratalmudic disciplines, philosophy and philology, into Provence and to popularize them. Thus do we find Kimḥi stepping in to complete the translation of Baḥya's *Duties of the Heart* after Ibn Tibbon had limited himself to translating the first chapter alone. It was only when this translation proved inadequate that Ibn Tibbon, with considerable soul searching, returned to the *Duties* and completed his own translation, prefacing his work with "a long discourse on intelligence and fools who undertake tasks incommensurate with their ability – a reference to Joseph Kimhi, as is clear from the immediately following paragraphs."[18]

The works which Kimḥi chose for translation, such as the *Duties* and the *Choice of Pearls*, were not of the most abstruse and were intended for a popular audience. Kimḥi himself was not a systematic philosopher; his *métier* lay in other disciplines. Yet he was led to this attempt to disseminate philosophical literature by his own belief in the veracity of the rationalist view of religion which, in the words of Baḥya ibn Paquda, maintained that:

> ... although in order of time, instruction based on tradition must necessarily precede knowledge obtained by the exercise of reason, inasmuch as learners must necessarily rely on what they are taught before they can obtain independent knowledge; yet it would show want of zeal for anyone to rely on tradition alone who can obtain certainty by the method of rational demonstration. Everyone who has the requisite capacity is in duty bound to investigate with his reason whatever can

[18] Twersky, *ibid.*, p. 199. Cf. M. Hyamson (ed.), *Duties of the Heart* (New York, 1941), II, p. [ii]. On the translation activity in Provence, see Twersky, *ibid.*, pp. 197f.

be so acquired, and to adduce proofs of it by the demonstration which deliberate judgment would support.[19]

Kimḥi sought to indoctrinate his reading public with this basic premise of the Jewish rationalist tradition that a belief in God based upon tradition alone is not sufficient but must be examined and supported by reason.[20] Expounding Proverbs 9:1, *Wisdom has built her house, she has hewn out her seven pillars*, Kimḥi explains that the first five pillars are the five senses and that the sixth pillar is that of second-hand knowledge or true reports of reliable witnesses *(haggadat ha-maggidim)* by which we can know that something is true even if we have not seen it ourselves.

The seventh pillar, however is the right hand pillar in which there is the greatest strength *(bo'az)*[21] and might and which is the support of all wisdom. Through it we acknowledge and know our Creator, be He blessed and exalted. This [is the sense by] which one ... observes an act and acknowledges the agent. [Thus] he may see a book which has been written without knowing the scribe through one of the senses which we mentioned above. Yet his writing bears witness as to whether he is skilled in his craft or not. Similarly, a house which has been built teaches about the builder. It is through this pillar that we acknowledge our Creator, blessed be He. Now someone may say that we acknowledge our Creator, through the sixth sense which is the reporting of reporters, such as their saying that we believe in [the existence of] towns and cities and districts without attaining a know-

[19] Baḥya ibn Paquda, Duties of the Heart, ed. Hyamson, I (New York, 1925), p. 10. Cf. p. 9. The second of the inward duties enumerated by Baḥya and the subject of the second chapter of his treatise is "the examination *(i'tibār, beḥinah)* of created things and God's abounding goodness towards them." See *Duties*, ed. Hyamson, II, pp. 1 et seq.

[20] Cf, the statements of Moses Maimonides, *Mishneh Torah, Hilkhot Yesode ha-Torah* II:2; cf. *Guide for the Perplexed*, I:34. See Talmage, *HUCA* XXXIX (1968), 177f.

[21] An allusion to the column of Solomon's temple named "Boaz." According to Scripture, Boaz was the name of the left column (I Kings 7:21).

ledge of them by sense perception. [This is achieved] only through reports which are undenied. Thus do we believe and acknowledge that the world has a Creator by virtue of people's reports [which] are undenied. The reply is that those who report concerning regions and districts [may do so] principally because some of them have seen them although some of them have not. Further, if they do not believe, they can go see [for themselves]. However, the root of the knowledge of the Creator is not vision, for all reporters, [from] first [to] last, are incompetent as far as seeing the Creator is concerned. Thus do we acknowledge His unity and know His existence through His works. From a world built without deficiency and founded with wisdom and knowledge can we acknowledge that one Creator created it and that God brought it into existence by His grace.[22]

This affirmation of the rationalist creed is found in the introduction to Kimḥi's *Sefer ha-Galui*, a grammatical work. It is included there apparently for the purpose of drawing an analogy between the priority of sciences in philosophic studies (first technology; second, astronomy, geometry, and medicine; third, theology) and in traditional studies (grammar, biblical exegesis, rabbinics). Thus while medicine may not be the most noble of the sciences, a knowledge of it is prerequisite to a full knowledge of metaphysics and theology.

Further, one may have achieved a knowledge of astrology or medicine, etc., being profound in one and not in others. Thus the expert in medicine can do in one moment that which a hundred star-gazers cannot do because of their ignorance of drugs. Similarly one expert in astronomy can pass a judgment concerning the constellations which a hundred physicians could not do because of their ignorance and incompetence with respect to the constellations. It has been said that the science of medicine is not complete and perfect without a knowledge

[22] *Sefer ha-Galui*, ed. Mathews, p. 1. On this passage, see Talmage, *HUCA* XXIX (1968), 182ff.

> of and acquaintance with the constellations [for the effect of the drugs is related to the particular astronomical configuration] ... It is so with the various crafts. That which a smith can achieve [by virtue of his expertise in his craft] in an instant, one hundred carpenters could not achieve. Similarly, in each craft, one is an expert in his own and ignorant of the others unless he has learned it.[23]

Thus each science, humble though it be, needs its specialists. Kimḥi's own specialization, as we have seen, was grammar and bible exegesis. From Kimḥi's introductory remarks to the *Sefer ha-Galui*, it may be seen that the profusion of grammatical studies which had appeared in Spain and the lack of agreement among them led Kimḥi who at the age of sixty had "spent most of his days in the study of grammar"[25] to attempt to reach some definitive conclusions in the works mentioned above. Further, the study of the grammatical aspects of Scripture *(diqduqeha)* was considered propadeutic for the study of its plain sense *(peshaṭeha)*.[26] Biblical study in Provence had been characterized in this period by a "preoccupation with midrash, operating on different levels and with different methods of interpretation."[27] The works of Moses the Preacher (early 11th c.) and similar midrashic compilations made their appearance from the beginning of the eleventh century and continued to do so for some time to come.[28] Yet unlike Northern France where alongside the midrashic compendia

[23] Sefer ha-Galui. p. 2.

[24] See Hirschfeld, *Lit. Hist.* and S. Baron, *Social and Religious History of the Jews* (Philadelphia, 1958), VII, pp. 3 et seq.

[25] *Sefer ha-Galui*, p. 2.

[26] *Ibid.*

[27] Twersky, *JWH*, XI (1968), p. 186, n. 3.

[28] Cf. A. Epstein, *R. Moses ha-Darshan* (Vienna, 1891); *Midrash Bereshit Rabbati*, ed. Ch. Albeck (Jerusalem, 1940); French tr., Jean Joseph Brierre-Narbonne (Paris, 1939).

of the Tosaphists[29] there were produced a number of commentaries which were concerned with revealing "the literal expositions which are daily being made evident",[30] Provence had produced no independent commentatorial activity based upon the method of *peshaṭ*. This gap was filled by Spanish outsiders who passed through having left their imprint clearly visible[32] or who, like Kimḥi, settled in Provence and established a whole school of native *pashṭanim*.[33]

Kimḥi's activities as translator, exegete, and grammarian led him to the role of defender of the faith against Christian antagonists.[34] Our literary records, both Latin and Hebrew, reveal a great deal of disputational activity in private debates between Jews and Christian prelates or apostates from Judaism which was characterized by great freedom of expression on

[29] See E. E. Urbach, *Ba'ale ha-Tosafot* (Jerusalem, 1955), passim. For a list of commentaries of the Tosaphists, see S. D. Sasson (ed.) *Moshav Zeqenim 'al ha-Torah* (London, 1959), pp. 520f.

[30] A phrase used by the dean of medieval Jewish biblical exegetes, R. Solomon b. Isaac (1040-1105), in a conversation with his grandson, R. Samuel ben Meir (1080-1158), in which the former expressed the wish for leisure to write new commentaries stressing the literal sense *(peshaṭ)*. See *Comm.* of Samuel ben Meir to Gen. 37:2, ed. D. Rosin (Breslau, 1881), p. 49.

[31] Joseph Kimḥi's son, David, was launched on his career as an exegete by the request of one of his father's students for a *peshaṭ* commentary to the Book of Chronicles. See his int. to Chron.

[32] Such as Abraham ibn Ezra (1088-1167). See J. L. Fleisher, "Rabbi 'Avraham 'ibn 'Ezra be-Ẓarefat", *Mi-mizraḥ u-Ma'arav*. IV (1930), 352-360; V (1931), 38-46, 217-224, 289-300.

[33] i. e. "literalists". Among his disciples in the field of exegesis are his son Moses (d. 1190?) and Menaḥem ben Simeon of Posquières. See M. Barol, *Menachem ben Simon aus Posquieres und sein Kommentar zu Jeremia und Ezechiel*, (Berlin, 1907), p. 4 et passim. Kimḥi's son David, who did not have the opportunity to study with R. Joseph because of the latter's death while David was still young, knew and studied his father's writings and the influence of R. Joseph is evident throughout the commentaries. See H. Cohen, *The Commentary of Rabbi David Kimhi on Hosea*, (New York, 1929), pp. xxxvii f.

[34] See L. I. Newman, "Joseph ben Isaac Kimhi as a Religious Controversialist", in *Jewish Studies in Memory of Israel Abrahams* (New York, 1927), pp. 365-372.

both sides.[35] Christian participants in the debates frequently found themselves disconcerted by the degree of initiative taken by Jews and by the extent to which they were prepared.[36] Writers in all fields evinced awareness of the Christian challenge and polemical remarks could be found anywhere from grammatical works, e.g. Kimḥi's own *Sefer ha-Galui*,[37] to philosophical works,[38] to poetry.[39] Biblical commentaries frequently dealt with Christological interpretations of Scripture and thereby functioned as parallels to Christian *testimonia*.[40] In addition, however, to all these literary genres where polemical remarks were introduced as the occasion demanded, there also existed special treatises intended as manuals for the potential disputant.

[35] *JbR*, p. xix; B. Blumenkranz, *Juifs et Chrétiens dans le Monde Occidentale* (Paris, 1960), pp. 220ff. Cf. the remarks of E. E. Urbach in "Études sur la Littérature Polémique au Moyen Age", *REJ* C(1935), 60f.: "Je veux bien admettre que certaines violences de langage soient à mettre exclusivement au compte de la rédaction, et qu'en fait ces propos n'aient jamais été exprimés devant un Chrétien.... Un fait psychologique aide aussi à expliquer ces propos parfois violents. Le besoin naturel de vengeance de ces gens harcelés et torturés n'avait trouvé dans la vie aucune satisfaction. C'est uniquement l'expression littéraire qui leur permettait de se soulager et de donner libre cours à leurs sentiments. Précisément dans les pays où les Juifs avaient le plus de liberté les sentiments de haine apparaissent le moins...." Yet he goes on to say, "Malgré tout cela, le fait est que, dans leurs discussions avec leurs adversaires chrétiens, les Juifs se sont permis beaucoup de libertés...."

[36] See the statement of Andrew of St. Victor, cited by B. Smalley, *Study of the Bible in the Middle Ages* (Notre Dame, 1964), p. 163; the ban of Bishop Odo of Paris against laymen's debating with Jews in S. Grayzel, *The Church and the Jews in the XIIIth Century*[2] (New York, 1966) pp. 300f.; J. Rosenthal, *Sefer Yosef ha-Meqanne* (Jerusalem, 1970), p. xvii; J. R. Marcus; *The Jew in the Medieval World* (New York, 1960), p. 42.

[37] *Sefer ha-Galui*, s.v. *'lm*, pp. 134f; par. 123, p. 54; D. Kimḥi, *Sefer ha-Shorashim*, s.v. *'lm*, ed. Berlin, 1847, p. 268.

[38] Thus does Saadia Gaon refute Christian doctrines in the *Beliefs and Opinions*. Cf. II:5, III:7, VIII:9 (ed. Rosenblatt, pp. 103ff., 158f., 319f.).

[39] See L. Zunz, *Die synagogale Poesie des Mittelalters*[2], (Berlin, 1919), pp. 437ff.

[40] Cf. J. Rosenthal, "Ha-Pulmos ha-'anti-noẓeri be-Rashi 'al ha-TaNaKH", *Meḥqarim* (Jerusalem, 1967), I, 213-235; *Sefer Yosef ha-Meqanne*, pp. xiii f.; Talmage, *HUCA*, XXXVIII (1967), 213-235; Cf. the remark of Joseph Kimḥi cited in the commentary of his son David to Ps. 22:30, ed. Schiller-Szinessy, Cambridge, 1883, pp. 69f.

The *Book of the Covenant* contests with the *Wars of the Lord (Milḥamot ha-Shem)* of Jacob ben Reuben the honor of being the first Hebrew polemical treatise written on the European continent.[41] However, unlike the *Wars*, which has survived in several manuscripts and has been critically edited,[42] the *Book of the Covenant* has been preserved only in that collection of polemical treatises known as the *Milḥemet Ḥovah* published at Constantinople in 1710.[43] The text itself is in as poor a condition as is its companion treatise, the so-called *Wikkuaḥ ha-RaDaQ (Disputation of R. David Kimḥi)*[44] It abounds in faults of style, dittographs, and non sequiturs. As has long been recognized, the concluding section, included in this translation, cannot be ascribed to Joseph Kimḥi at all,[45] while the text

[41] *JbR*, p. xxi. There has been considerable bibliographic confusion concerning Kimḥi's alleged authorship of other polemical works. This has been thoroughly surveyed by L. I. Newman in "Joseph ... Kimḥi ... as Controversialist". See above, n. 34.

[42] *JbR*, pp. xxv f.

[43] 18b-38a. The original pagination of the *MḤ* is indicated in brackets in the translation. The text was reprinted with excessive "emendations" by J. D. Eisenstein in his *Oẓar Wikkuḥim* (New York, 1928), pp. 67-78. A new edition of the Hebrew text will appear in my *Wikkuḥe Mishpaḥat Qimḥi* to be published in the *Dorot* series of Mossad Bialik.

[44] See F. Talmage, "An Hebrew Polemical Treatise: Anti-Cathar and Anti-Orthodox", *HTR*-LXI (1967), 323.

[45] A. Geiger, *Parschandata* (Leipzig, 1855), pp. 212f.; *Qevuẓat Ma'amarim* (Warsaw, 1910), p. 213; "Proben Jued. Verteidigung gegen christliche Angriffe"; *Deutscher Volkskalendar und Jahrbuch*, I (1851), 63f.; E. Blueth, "Joseph Qimchi und seine Grammatik", *Magazin für die Wissenschaft des Judentums,* XVIII (1891), 206. In addition to the fact that this material does not follow the dialogue format of the *SB*, the following points are to be noted:
a) R. Eleazar ben Samuel, who has been indentified with R. Eleazar of Metz (d. 1198), author of the *Sefer Yere'im*, is cited as grandfather of the author. See J. Rosenthal, "Sifrut ha-wikkuaḥ ha-'anti-noẓerit 'ad sof ha-me'ah ha-shtem 'esreh", *'Areshet* I, p. 138;
b) there is a reference to Joseph Kara (ca. 1070-1140) whom apparently neither Joseph Kimḥi nor his son David knew. Cf. H. Cohen, *Commentary*, p. xxxv;
c) the exile is twice stated as having lasted more than 1200 years which set the earliest possible date of composition at 1270. See however H. H. Ben Sasson, "Yiḥud 'am yisra 'el le-da'at bene ha-me'ah ha-shtem 'esreh", *Peraqim* II, (Jerusalem, 1971), p. 86, n. 215.

itself contains two obvious interpolations.[46] Indeed, some have thought that the ascription of any of this material to Kimḥi is to be denied.[47] However, this extreme position is not tenable. The remainder of the material would seem to be genuine, if corrupted, from the fact of its correspondence to citations of the *Book of the Covenant* in other works.[48] It remains to be noted that the text in its present condition is probably incomplete since at least one passage, referred to by R. Joseph's son, R. David,[49] is missing.

It would appear from Kimhi's introductory statement (p. 27) that he was concerned primarily with a defense against apostates from Judaism who were trying to evangelize their former correligionists.[50] The treatise is thus couched as a dialogue between a *ma'amin*, i.e. a *fidelis*, and a *min*,[51] an *infidelis*.

[46] The passage from the disputation of Moses Naḥmanides at Barcelona in 1263 (p.59) see *Kitve ha-RaMBaN*, ed. Chavel, Jerusalem, 1963, II, 317; O. S. Rankin, *Jewish Religious Polemic* (Edinburgh, 1956), pp. 202f. and the passage on p. 53 ascribed to Isaac Halevi who has been indentified with R. Isaac ben Judah Halevi, the author of the *Pa'aneaḥ Raza* (late 13th c.). See S. Poznanski, *Perush al Yeḥezqe'el u-tere 'asar le-rabi 'Eli'ezer mi-Belgenzi* (Warsaw, 1909-11), pp. cvi-cvii. He may be alternatively indentified with R. Isaac Halevi, the teacher of R. Solomon ben Isaac. See A. Aptowitzer, *Mavo le-Sefer RaBi'aH* (Jeruzalem, 1936), p. 367.

[47] A. Levy, *Die Exegese bei den Französischen Israeliten von 10 bis 14 Jahrhundert* (Leipzig, 1873), p. 74; S. Steinschneider in Ersch und Gruber, sec. II, vol. XXVII, p. 410, n. 33.

[48] Kimḥi himself mentioned the *SB* in his *Sefer ha-Galui* (p. 135) where it is stated that the *SB* will follow the arrangement of a dialogue between a *ma'amin* and a *min* and cites the introductory verses to the *SB* missing in the *MḤ*. The discussion of the word *'almah* and of Isa. 7:14ff. (*Sefer ha-Galui*, pp. 134f.) substantially agrees with that found in *SB* (pp. 53ff.) as does that of Dan. 9:24ff. (*Sefer ha-Galui*, pp. 54f.; *SB*, pp. 49ff.). The references to the *SB* in David Kimhi's comm. to Gen. 1:26 and Isa. 7:14ff. correspond to our present text (cf. *Sefer ha-Galui*, pp. 134f.), while R. David's remarks on Isa. 9:5, Ps. 22:2, 72:1, 72:8, 87:4, 110:1 show the influence of the *SB*.

[49] *Comm*. of David Kimḥi, Isa. 52:13, ed. Guadalajara, 1481.

[50] On apostasy in medieval Europe, see B. Blumenkranz, *Juifs et Chrétiens*, pp. 138ff.; J. Katz, *Exclusiveness and Tolerance* (Oxford 1961), pp. 67ff.; S. Baron, *Soc. and Rel. Hist.*, V, pp. 112f. On polemical treatises written by apostates, see Baron, *Soc. and Rel. Hist.*, IX, pp. 292f.

[51] On *min* in rabbinic literature, see R. T. Herford, *Christianity in Talmud and Midrash* (London, 1907), pp. 361 et seq.

Kimḥi, who was fond of giving his works biblical titles, chose the name *Book of the Covenant* (Exod. 24:7) probably as an allusion to his attempt to bring back those who had abandoned the covenant.

The dialogue form was one of the most common formats for the polemical treatise, in both the Christian and Jewish traditions,[52] and such dialogues frequently reflect debates which actually took place. While the introduction to the work would seem to indicate that the *Book of the Covenant* is not the protocol of an actual disputation,[53] the echoes of such disputations are heard in the give and take. Frequently one hears exclamations of exasperation expressing the tension of a live debate. "How have I listened to your words and contemplated your speech!" (p.38) "Now finish your words!" (p.32) "How can you!" (p.45) "All things are difficult!" (p.53) The immediacy of the debate is suggested too by the undercurrent of the Romance vernacular in the Hebrew of the dialogue.[54]

The *Book of the Covenant* presents a picture of Judaism entirely consistent with the outlook of Kimḥi and his contemporaries. Just as it was presented to a Jewish audience, so was it depicted to a Christian – a religion in harmony with rational criteria. The theme of the reasonability of Judaism runs as a *Leitmotiv* throughout the disputational literature of the period. In the *Kuzari* of Kimḥi's contemporary, Judah

[52] See e.g. the contemporary *Wars of the Lord (Milḥamot ha-Shem)* on the Jewish side and the eleventh century *Disputatio Judaei cum Christiano* of Gilbert Crispin or the *Dialogus* of Petrus Alphonsi.

[53] See *JbR*, p. xxii.

[54] The preposition *min* is used several times in the sense of "concerning, about" reflecting Latin or Provençal *de (mi-shabbat mah tomeru, modim me'avotenu u-mi-mosheh rabbenu u-mi-kol nevi'enu)*. The Hebrew *biqqesh* is also used in the sense of *petere (mi she-rozeh la-ha'amin lo yevaqqesh divre yeshu)*. The text contains only six *le'azim* or vernacular expressions, three of which are corrupted in the *MH* text: *figura (pygwr')*; *batisme (btismy)*; *ped de la letra* (?), cf. n. 37 to text; *dialectica (rylyqt')*; *duc (dwq)*; *evangèli ('wrgly)*.

Halevi, the pagan king of the Khazar nation in search of the proper mode of action, is confronted with representatives of philosophy, Christianity, Islam, and Judaism. While his initial objections to Judaism grow into an encounter which eventually brings about his conversion, his potential dialogue with Christianity is abruptly curtailed after he hears an exposition of the Christian creed. "I see here no logical conclusion", replies the king, "*nay, logic rejects most of what thou sayest* .... As for me, I cannot accept these things, because they come upon me suddenly not having grown up in them. My duty is to investigate further."[55] The verdict is then that Christianity is a faith acceptable only to one who has been given it with his mother's milk and whose mysteries have been impressed upon his consciousness from earliest childhood.

That "logic rejects most of what thou sayest" is the cry which reverberates throughout the *Book of the Covenant*, be it in connection with a syllogistic refutation of a Christian dogma or in the context of the denunciation of a Christological interpretation of a biblical passage. Whereas the Christian remarks, "Whoever wishes to have faith should not scrutinize the words of Jesus ..." (p.32), the Jew insists, "Why do you not subject your belief to reason in an honest manner? [Scripture] speaks to a mature man, one who knows how to scrutinize his faith so that he will not err". (p.65) Whereas the Christians have taken the words of Scripture and "have explained them senselessly and have turned from the way of truth", (p.27) Kimḥi proposes to "begin by the grace of God to search and investigate by the paths of reason and to

[55] *Kuzari* I; 5, trans. Hirschfeld, p. 42. Another contemporary of Kimḥi, Jacob ben Reuben, begins his polemical work, *Wars of the Lord*, with a chapter "On Proofs Brought from Reason". Commenting on the Christian's statement of creed, the Jew remarks, "All the philosophers and all rationalists (*ḥakhme ha-sekhel*) scoff at you and question this". (*JbR*, p. 8)

answer with understanding and knowledge". (p.28) With respect to the belief in the incarnation, the Jew claims, "I do not profess this belief which you profess, for *my reason does not allow me* to diminish the greatness of God ...." (p.37) The exasperation of the Jew with his adversary is expressed in such cries as "How you have erred from the path of reason!" (p.30) or "God save us from this faith and anything resembling it"!. (p.64) In this context, Kimḥi's knowledge of Jewish philosophical literature comes to the fore. Thus familiar arguments for the unity of God are used to combat the notion of the Trinity,[56] while rationalizations of anthropomorphism culled from the philosophical sources serve as a basis for the denial of the Christian claim that God transferred his inheritance from Israel to the Church.[57]

It was expected too that the Bible, as well as theological dogmas, ultimately had to "make sense." "Scripture speaks to those who are intelligent and capable of understanding it". (p.42) It demands that reason be employed in understanding it but it will never tax the limits of reason. (See p.30.)

The Christian's ultimate reply to this is an accusation that the Jew adheres only to the "letter"; he does not realize that the text is to be read as *figura*.[58] (See p.46f.)

[56] See n. 30 to text.

[57] See nn. 30, 31 to text.

[58] Thus does Kimḥi's contemporary, Bartholemew, bishop of Exeter (d. 1184), write in his *Dialogue against the Jews*: "The chief cause of disagreement between ourselves and the Jews seems to me to be this: they take all the Old Testament literally, wherever they can find a literal sense, unless it gives a manifest witness to Christ. Then they repudiate it, saying that it is not in the Hebrew Truth, that is in their books, or they refer it to some fable, as that they are still awaiting its fulfillment, or they escape by some other serpentine wile, when they feel themselves hard pressed. They will never accept allegory, except when they have no other way out." Bartholemew continues: "*We* interpret not only the words of Scripture, but the things done, and the deeds themselves, in a mystical sense, yet in such a way that the freedom of allegory may in no wise nullify, either history in the

To this the "believer" replies that "the Torah is not [to be taken] altogether literally or altogether figuratively ..." (See p. 47.)

Our author had a broad acquaintance with Christian exegesis and comes to grips with a number of christological *loci classici*, among them Gen. 1:2, 1:26f., 18:1ff., 49:10; Deut. 18:15; Isa. 7:14, 9:5f.; Ps. 22:2, 72, 87:4, 110; Dan. 9:24ff. As did others of his contemporaries, he combatted the "corruptions" of the Vulgate[59] and Jerome[60] and even made reference to a "Book of Origen" upon which the translation of Jerome was said to be based.

One of the principal gambits used in medieval disputations between the Church and the Synagogue was the attempt of each to claim the right to the title *Verus Israel*. The Jews maintained that God never annulled the original election, while the Christians asserted that the birthright had passed from Israel in the flesh to Israel in the spirit, the Church.[61] This debate was carried out on many levels. One of these was the philological, in which the Church attempted the exegesis of Hebrew names for the Jewish People (Israel, Judah, Ephraim, etc.) to prove that they really applied to Christianity. It is on such a discussion that the *Book of the Covenant* breaks off: "When you find a consolation for Israel, they say, 'We are the sons of Jacob.' When they find a consolation for Judah, they say to you ..."[62]

events, or proper understanding of the words of Scripture". (Cited in Smalley, *Study*, pp. 170f.) Yet while "allegory" did not rule out "history", most commandments in their literal sense were considered abrogated.

[59] On Jewish knowledge of the Vulgate in this period, see Talmage, *HTR* LX (1967), 326, n. 19.

[60] Jerome is mentioned as a corrupter of Scripture by Kimḥi's contemporary, Jacob ben Reuben, and his son David. See n. 59.

[61] See M. Simon, *Verus Israel* (Paris, 1948), p. 165; B. Blumenkranz, *Juifs et Chrétiens*, pp. 272ff.; Talmage, *HUCA* XXXVIII (1967), *ibid.*

[62] See n. 82 to text; Talmage, *HUCA* XXXVIII (1967), *ibid.*

More to the point, however, was the contention that the Israel of God were known not so much by their name [as] by their fruits. Those worthy of bearing the name "Israel" are those who behave as the people of God ought. The medieval Jewish polemicist contrasted the way of life of the Jew, devoted to learning and piety, with that of the Christians who do not even "observe the Law of Grace in many of its aspects and fight and behave violently towards each other".[63] Thus does R. Joseph rehearse the high moral quality of Jewish life (pp. 32f.) and the Jew's dedication to study and to the education of his children, (p. 32) praised even in contemporary Christian literature. He stresses that Jews not only refrain from anti-social behavior but indeed in their dealings with each other, they are the paradigm of the just society (p.33).[66]

A standard countercharge levelled by Christianity against the Jews was the claim that Jews exact usury in direct contradiction to the law of the Torah.[67] R. Joseph Kimhi's Jew replies in standard fashion that this prohibition applies only to fellow Jews (p.34f.).

While Christians might be guilty of certain moral deficiencies, Christian polemicists maintained that true moral per-

[63] *JbR*, p. 146.

[64] See B. Smalley, *Study*, p. 78

[65] Cf. the striking parallel in the passage published by E. E. Urbach, *REJ* C(1936), 66. See also Justin's *Dialogue* X, XVII, CXIII (ed. A. L. Williams, pp. 20, 36, 224); *AJ*, p. 382; *JbR*, pp. 91, 146; H. Crescas, *Biṭṭul 'iqqare dat ha-noẓerim* in Eisenstein, *Oẓar*, p. 297; *HUCA* XXXVIII (1967), 225. On social criticism in religious polemics, see H. H. Ben Sasson, "Yiḥud 'am Yisrael ...", *Peraqim* II (Jerusalem, 1971), pp. 86ff.; J. Rosenthal, "Hagganah ve-Hatqafah be-Sifrut ha-Wikkuaḥ shel Yeme ha-Benayim" in the forthcoming *Proceedings of the Fifth World Congress of Jewish Studies* (Jerusalem, 1971).

[66] Cf. the statement of Abraham Maimonides, *Comm.* to Exod. 19:6, ed. Weisenberg (London, 1959), p. 302. See H. H. Ben Sasson, *Toledot Yisrael bi-Yeme ha-Benayim* (Tel Aviv, 1969), p. 166.

[67] See n. 19 to text.

fection is achieved only through the religious vocation and that, in the words of the *min*, "there are people among them who separate themselves in their way of life from the world and its pleasures and dwell in forests and deserts in affliction all their days", (p.34). Thus did Judah Halevi's Khazar king express astonishment that there were not "more hermits and ascetics among you than among other people."[68] His interlocutor reminds him, of course, that "man cannot approach God except by means of deeds commanded by him".[69] Joseph Kimḥi's exponent of Judaism is singularly unimpressed by the Gentile's claims (p.35).[70] With respect to celibacy, frequently derided in Jewish polemical literature,[71] Kimḥi makes the customary assertion that "it is well known that your priests and bishops who do not marry are fornicators" (p.35).

THE ADDITIONS TO THE *BOOK OF THE COVENANT*

The material appended to the *Book of the Covenant*[72] in the *Milḥemet Ḥovah* bears a strong resemblance to the work of R. Joseph. Like Kimḥi, the author of the additions stresses that "the root of belief is implanted in the waters of reason and understanding, wisdom and true knowledge", and cites his grandfather[72] as having set forth "the sure, concise arguments ... which [invoke] the power of reason. ..." (p.69).

Like R. Joseph too, the author stresses that the actual way of life of the Jewish people is the greatest testimony to the permanence of the covenant. Thus, unlike the Trinitarian Christians, the Jews have been "committed to His divinity and His unity over above any other commandment which

[68] *Kuzari* II:45; Hirschfeld, p. 111.
[69] *Kuzari* II:46; Hirschfeld, p. 111.
[70] See below, p.35; n. 21 to text.
[71] See n. 21 to text.
[72] See above, p.18, n. 45.

God gave us through Moses our teacher" (p.71). Again, unlike the Christians "who make images and bow down before them", the Jews accept the prohibition against "worshipping other gods and ... making images" (p.72). Indeed, "in these more than twelve hundred years that our exile has lasted, we have not forgotten His holy Torah",[73] to the extent that "even the women know the commandments and precepts and are expert in the subtleties of rabbinic tradition" (p.78). In return for this,

> we see today with our very eyes His many deeds of kindness and His great mercy in that He has not ceased to act in righteousness and truth with this people these twelve hundred years. Further, He preserved our exile [brought about] by our iniquities and did not abandon us or break His covenant with us (p.78).

The author of the additions evinced a sense of irony in his remarks which is especially reminiscent of the anti-Christian polemics of the Northern French Tosaphists.[74] This is seen in the comments concerning the crucifixion in which the author attempts to show that while the Jews were indeed instrumental in the crucifixion, their intentions were sound and they should consequently be praised rather than blamed.[75] In a similar vein is the passage (p.73) which claims that Mary should have given birth to a male and female to correspond to the fact that both Adam and Eve sinned, since God's justice operates on the principle of measure for measure.

[73] On the dating, see n. 45 above.

[74] This is especially evident in the *Sefer Yosef ha-Meqanne*. See also the passages cited and translated by E. E. Urbach, "Études", *REJ* C(1935), 49-77.

[75] Note the comments ascribed to R. Joseph Kara (p.68), the play on *meyashsherim* (p.76), and the comment on p.64. Cf. H. H. Ben Sasson, "Yiḥud", *Peraqim* II, pp. 29ff.

THE BOOK OF THE COVENANT COMPOSED BY THE SAGE R. JOSEPH KIMḤI OF BLESSED MEMORY.

Strengthen the weak hands and make firm the feeble knees. Say to those who are of a fearful heart: "Be strong, fear not." Your God will come with vengeance, with the recompense of God He will come and save you. (Isa. 35:3f.) *But you,* [19a] *take courage, and do not let your hands be weak, for your work shall be rewarded.* (II Chron. 15:7.) *Be strong and let your heart take courage, all you that wait for the Lord.* (Ps. 31:25.) *The spirit of the Lord speaks through me; His word is upon my tongue* (II Sam. 23:2).

I have observed that the children of the impudent among our people[1] have audaciously proclaimed all manner of falsehood and nonsense. Their foolishness and stupidity have completely misled them and their ignorance has enticed them into misinterpreting the words of the living God, the words of the prophets, and to apply them in an improper fashion to the matter of Jesus the Nazarene. They have explained them senselessly and have turned from the way of truth.

One of my students has requested me to assemble and collect all the visions and prophecies in the Torah, Prophets,

[1] The phrase "the children of the impudent among our people", taken from Dan. 11:14, was traditionally applied to Jesus and his disciples. See S. Krauss, *Das Leben Jesu nach Jüdischen Quellen* (Berlin, 1902), pp. 76, 80, 121, *et passim;* Rashi, *a.l.; Josippon,* ed. Mantua, ch. 63; J. Rosenthal (ed.), *Sefer Yosef ha-Meqanne* (Jerusalem, 1970), p. 15; G. Cohen, *The Book of Tradition of Abraham ibn Daud* (New York, 1968), p. xxxix, n. 114; M. Maimonides, *Epistle to Yemen,* ed. A.S. Halkin (New York, 1951), p. iv; J. Rosenthal, *Meḥqarim* (Jerusalem, 1967), I, 115.

and Writings, in which there are [contained] refutations against the heretics and deniers *('epiqorsin)* who polemize against our faith. I have seen fit to fulfil his request. In this there will be found much benefit, in that it will add [to the glory of] the faith of the God of Israel. The wise man will grow stronger and *those who are wise* shall understand and *shall shine as the brightness of the firmament, and those who turn many to righteousness are like the stars for ever and ever* (Dan. 12:3). I shall begin by the grace of God to search and investigate by the paths of reason and to answer with understanding and knowledge.

They profess and believe in the Trinity-Father, Son, and Spirit – and claim that the Creator is the Father of all and that He created the entire world. At the beginning of the Book of Genesis, it states, *and the Spirit of the Lord hovered over the face of the waters* (Gen. 1:2). Hence: Father and Spirit.[2] We reply: I believe that wisdom corroborates them and reason is on their side. He is the Father of the world, having engendered it and brought it into being *ex nihilo*, and the [existence of] the Holy Spirit [may be seen in this verse also]. But who will constrain me to believe that he has a son [in the same way that] reason constrains me [to believe] in the Father and Spirit?[3]

The *min*[4] said: You have judged wisely and spoken well by accepting belief in the Father and the Spirit, [both] from Scripture and from reason. I cannot prove [the existence of the Son] from reason, but in any event I can from Scripture.

[2] i.e. the words "Spirit" and "Lord" refer to the Spirit and the Father.

[3] The Christian argument is not as complete here as in the early writers and in the anonymous treatise of 1166 cited in *AJ* in which the Hebrew *bereshit* was actually translated or at least interpreted as *in filio*. See *AJ*, p. 396. Cf. the reference to the *Dialogue of Jason and Papiscus* in *AJ*, p. 29; Jerome, *Hebr. Quaest. in Gen.*, *PL* XXIII, 987; Isidore, *De Fide Cath.*, PL LXXXIII, 458 ("in principio Filius agnosticur"). See also Saadia ben Joseph, *Beliefs and Opinions*, II:6; *JbR*, pp. 40, 42.

[4] See introduction.

All the prophets spoke and prophesied concerning the Son.... [19b] I believe in the words of the prophets. Isaiah said, *A child is born to us, a son is given to us, and the* principatus *will be upon his shoulders; and his name will be called Wonderful Counsellor, Mighty God, Everlasting Father, Prince of Peace* (Isa. 9:5). It is not possible that these names refer to a human being. Therefore, [this] has constrained me to believe in the Son.

[*The ma'amin said*:] There is an error in the verse which you cited [which was introduced] by Jerome, you translator. The pointing does not indicate a reading of *he shall be called God*, but *the Wonderful Counsellor, Mighty God, Everlasting Father shall call his name the prince of peace.*[5] This is Hezekiah the righteous whom God called prince of peace. [This is so for the following reason:] Sects, wars, and dissensions had proliferated in the time of his father Ahaz, for Pekah the son of Remaliah and Rezin, king of Aram, warred against him, defeated him, and destroyed his land.[6] The prophet Isaiah announced to him that a child had been born, upon whose shoulder would rest the dominion of the House of David. We have found it stated explicitly in Chronicles that Hezekiah had already been born.[7] These names were mentioned according to the circumstances: *Wonderful*, for He wrought wonders with him; *Counsellor*, for He counselled him to walk in the ways of the Lord, for his father was wicked; *Mighty God*, for He caused him to grow mighty over his enemies; *Everlasting Father*, for He added fifteen years to his life,[8] for He is the Master and

[5] The Vulgate renders "vocabitur" which assumes a reading of "wayyiqqare" while the Masoretic text reads "wayiqra" in the active. See Jerome, *Comm. on* Isa., a.l., *PL* XXIV, 127f. Kimḥi's interpretation of the verse is based on Rashi. See H. Hailprin, *Rashi and the Christian Scholars* (Pittsburgh, 1963), p. 310, n. 249.

[6] II Kings 16:5f.

[7] According to II Chron. 29:1, Hezekiah was twenty-five years old upon ascending the throne.

[8] II Kings 20:6.

Father of eternity.[9] Further, if, as you say, he spoke this verse in reference to the Son, he should have made this quite explicit, for in the case of a non-rational doctrine, the prophets would set it forth clearly in a plain statement. Who will believe that the Holy One blessed be He entered the womb of a woman and took on flesh? Is it not said concerning flesh: *He remembered that they were but flesh, a wind that passes and does not come again*, (Ps. 78:39). Who will believe that the Lord of the world was *born of woman, of few clays and full of trouble* (Job 14:1)? Thus I am not constrained to believe in the Son. Scripture says too: *My spirit shall not remain in man forever since he is flesh*, (Gen. 6:3). You have denied this text.

The *min* said: Do you not know and have you not heard that because Adam sinned, all his progency go [20a] to Gehenna[10] and are punished (for Adam's sin.) Therefore, He wanted to descend to earth and take on flesh in Mary's womb to save the world. In His great humility, He came to earth to take the righteous from Gehenna, because for the guilt of Adam, they went there upon their death, and for his crime, He cursed the earth, as it is said: *Cursed be the earth because of you* (Gen. 3:17).

The *ma'amin* said: How you have erred from the path of reason! *Does God pervert judgment? Does the Almighty pervert justice?* (Job 8:3), so as to bring the righteous to Gehenna for the sin of Adam? Does not Scripture say, *Parents shall not be put to death for children* (Deut. 24:16)?[11] I say further: You claim that Jesus saved the world from the day he came, but

[9] See Hailprin, *Rashi*, pp. 169ff; Comm. of Joseph Kara, Isa. 9:5; *JbR*, p. 89; Ibn Ezra interpreted the names in a manner similar to that of Kimḥi but applied them to the child. Kimḥi, with a specifically polemical intent, followed Rashi who referred them to God. Kimḥi's exegesis is found in the commentary of his son, *a.l.*

[10] Heb. *Gehinnom*, the most common Hebrew term for hell.

[11] The continuation of the verse is intended: *and children shall not be put to death for parents*.

he accomplished nothing which can actually be seen. Scripture says: *In anguish shall you eat of it* (Gen. 3:17) *and in pain shall you bear children* (Gen. 3:16), and it is so to this day.[12] This which is manifest has not been remedied and you say it has been remedied [....] I do not see from your words that after he underwent the torments of death, the righteous left Gehenna. I shall bring you a proof from your Gospel that your words are false. Jesus said to his disciples: *There was a very rich man dressed in garments of silk and purple. On his table, were all kinds of food. A poor man, Lazarus by name, who was hungry and thirsty, came to his table. He had no mercy upon him and gave him neither bread to eat nor water to drink. Lazarus died afterwards and the angels took him and placed him in Abraham's bosom. Afterwards, that rich man died and they brought him to Gehenna. He raised his eyes and saw Lazarus in Abraham's bosom and said to him "My father, have mercy upon me and tell Lazarus that I am condemned to a great flame." Abraham answered him "Remember, my son, when you were very rich. Now he is rich and you are poor." He also said to Abraham "I have five brothers and if one of you goes there, let him tell them not to do things which would cause* [*them to suffer*] *this flame." Abraham said to him "They have indeed the words of the prophets. Let them hear and accept them. If they do not hearken* [20b] *to them, they will believe no one."* (Cf. Luke 16:19-31) How shall we believe that the righteous are in Gehenna according to this? You believe that three days after his death he descended to Gehenna and brought the righteous out. This contradicts the doctrine in which you believe, for all your words *are worthless and empty* (Isa. 30:7) and you have no reply to this.[13]

[12] Cf. Disp. of Naḥmanides, in Rankin, *Jew. Rel. Polemic* (Edinburgh, 1956), p. 190; J. Rosenthal, *Meḥqarim* (Jerusalem, 1967), I, 437.

[13] The parable of Lazarus is brought later as a refutation of the notion of the suffering of the righteous in Limbo in the *Wikkuaḥ ha-RaDaQ, MH,* f. 16a; *HTR*

The *min* said: Whoever wishes to have faith should not scrutinize[14] the words of Jesus even though they be acceptable to reason.

You have neither faith nor deeds, dominion nor sovereignty, for you have lost all. I have many verses in your Torah which support me in this belief. Now finish your words.

The *ma'amin* said: Know that all the good which a man achieves in this world is of two kinds: good works and faith. If I can attribute good works and faith to the Jews, then they have everything. I shall begin to tell of these good works which you cannot deny and I shall start with the Ten Commandments: *I* [*am the Lord*, etc.] (Exod. 20:2). The Jews declare God's unity; *You shall have no* [*other gods beside Me.*] (v. 3). The Jews do not make idols; *You shall not take* [*the name of the Lord in vain*] (v. 7) There is no nation in the world which avoids vain oaths as does Israel: *Remember* [*the Sabbath day*] (v. 8). Only Israel keeps the Sabbath; Honor [your father ...] (v. 12); likewise, *You shall not murder, You shall not commit adultery* (v. 13). Similarly, there are no murderers or adulterers among them. Oppression and theft are not as widespread among Jews as among Christians who rob people on the highways and hang them and sometimes gouge out their eyes. You cannot establish any of these things with respect to the Jews. These Jews and Jewesses who are modest in all their deeds, raise their children, from the youngest to the oldest, in the study of the Torah. If they hear a vile word from the mouth [of a child], they beat him and chastise him so that he would no longer swear with his lips. They train him too to pray every day. If they hear that he has become accustomed to swearing, they will keep him from [doing] so.

(LX, 1967), p. 343; and by Profiat Duran in *Kelimat ha-Goyim*. See the edition of Poznanski in *ha-Ẓofeh* III, p. 153.

[14] Heb. *yevaqqesh,* reflecting the Latin *petere*.

Their daughters, with modesty, are not be seen about nor found wanton like the daughters of the gentiles who go out everywhere to streetcorners. [21a] The Holy One, blessed be He, has prevented all this [among the Jews]. Are you not then ashamed and embarrassed to say that you are a good people since you regularly and publicly encourage these sins. [You are] not from a people that will prevent this sort of thing. On the contrary, [your children] become accustomed to sin. [The sins] may be light as cobwebs in the windows of a house. Yet [such cobwebs] keep out the light [as] these sins keep the light from you.

I tell you further that whenever a Jew stops at the home of his fellow for a day or two or [even] a year, he will take no payment for food from him. This is so with all the Jews in the world who act toward their brethren with compassion. If they see their brother a captive, they ransom him; [if] naked, they clothe him and do not allow him to go about begging. They send him provisions in secret. You see with your own eyes that the Christian goes out on the highways to meet travellers – not to honor them – but to swindle them and take all their provisions from them. No one can deny that all these good traits which I mentioned are found among the Jews and [that] their opposites [are found] among Christians. Further, the Jews keep their Sabbaths and festivals conscientiously, while the Christians do all manner of work and travel about even on Sunday which is their holy [day]. What more can you ask for in the way of good deeds found among Jews and bad deeds found among Christians?[15]

He answered: You are right in part. Yet what good are their deeds if they have no faith? I shall show you other deeds which you do that are contrary to religion. You lend

[15] On this passage, see introduction.

with usury,[16] although David said *Who will dwell in your tabernacle? He who has not lent his money with usury* (Ps. 15:1,5). I shall show you other good deeds which (Christians) [Jews] do. There are people among them who separate themselves in their way of life from the world and from its pleasures and dwell in forests and deserts in affliction all their days.

The *ma'amin* said: [21b] Usury, to which you refer is mentioned in the Torah of Moses: *You may take usury on loans to foreigners but not on loans to your countrymen* (Deut. 23:21). Thus when David said *he who has not lent his money with usury* (Ps. 15:5), he reiterated what had been forbidden them. Do you not see that although Scripture said *You shall not kill*![17] (Exod. 20:13), David killed thousands from among the nations? This is because *you shall not kill* means that you shall not kill one who is innocent. Similarly, *he who has not lent his money with usury* is to be interpreted with reference to what the Torah forbade. There was no need for David to refer to this since Moses had already stated it. The Jews are indeed scrupulous about usury and the taking of interest from their brethren as the Torah forbade. They are also very scrupulous about *'avaq ribbit* (the dust of usury).[18] A Jew will not lend his brother wheat, wine, or any commodity on a term basis in order to increase his profit, while you, who have disdained usury, sell all commodities to your brethren on a term basis at twice the price. You should be ashamed to say that you do not lend with usury for this is enormous usury. Furthermore, many gentiles clearly lend on interest to [both] Jews

[16] Heb. *ribbit* is generally translated as "usury" here in accordance with the Vulgate and ecclesiastical tradition.

[17] Heb. *lo tirzaḥ* "you shall not murder", here translated as "you shall not kill", in accordance with the Latin "Non occides".

[18] That which resembles usury. See *JE,* XII, 389.

and gentiles, although Jews do not lend to their fellow Jews.[19]

Now with respect to your statement that there are many holy people[20] among them (the gentiles) who separate themselves from this world in their lifetime, [it must be said] that they are one in a thousand or ten thousand, while the rest are contaminated by the ways of the world. It is well known that your priests and bishops who do not marry are fornicators. Now when Israel were in their land, there were few righteous men among them. Because there were many wicked men, Nebuchadnezzar came and exiled and slaughtered them. Thus David said *O God, gentiles have invaded Your domain, etc. They have given the corpses of Your servants to the fowl of heaven for food, the flesh of Your righteous ones to the beasts of the earth* (Ps. 79:1f.). What good will it do you then if you have one man in a million who is conscientious about serving his God? Even more so, I do not believe that one who has isolated himself in the forest is perfect in his actions and his belief.[21] Yet if he *is* perfect in his actions, they will do him no good if his faith is not perfect.

The *min* said: [22a] All the good deeds to which you referred will do you no good since you do not believe that Jesus became incarnate through Mary in order to save the world.

[19] The question of Jewish exacting of interest from gentiles appeared in practically every medieval disputation. For a comprehensive survey of the problem, see J. Rosenthal, "Ribbit min ha-nokhri" in *Meḥqarim,* I, 253-323; cf. M. Stein, "A Disputation on Money-lending between Jews and Gentiles in Meir b. Simeon's *Milhemeth Miṣwah*", *JJS* X (1959), p. 52; *HUCA* XXXVIII (1967), pp. 225f.

[20] Heb. *qedeshim.*

[21] Celibacy and monasticism, altogether foreign to the Jewish mind, was frequently derided in the literature. See *Nestor ha-Komer* (ed. Berliner), p. 8; Abraham Maimonides, *Comm.* to Exod. 19:6, ed. Weisenberg (London, 1959), p. 302; E.E. Urbach, "Études sur la Littérature Polémique au Moyen Age", *REJ* C(1935), pp. 69f; B. Blumenkranz, "Die jüdischen Beweisgründe im Religionsgespräch mit den Christen in den christlichlateinischen Sonderschriften den 5. bis 11. Jahrhunderts", *TZ* IV (1948), p. 146; Rosenthal, *Meḥqarim,* I, 452, n. 93; H. H. Ben Sasson, *Toledot yisra'el bi-yeme ha-benayim* (Tel Aviv, 1969), p. 167.

Works follow faith but faith does not follow works. Even though there is evildoing among the Christians, they have sound faith so that they will fully repent and be received by the Creator by virtue of the faith which they profess. However, the actions of you do not believe in Him are in vain and your deeds are for naught. You labor for no purpose and your efforts are wasted. If you sin, your repentance will not help you since you do not believe in Him.

The *ma'amin* said: How you rely on naught and depend on vanity! I believe in the Creator of the world *Who does not tire or weary and Whose understanding cannot be fathomed* (Isa. 40:28), the God in Whom Adam believed and the God in Whom all the ancients believed – Abraham, Isaac, Jacob, Moses, Aaron, David, Solomon, and all the righteous and prophets before the coming of Jesus. All of them believed in the Creator of the world but did not believe in Jesus since he had not [yet] come into the world. Now that he has come and appeared to the world, you believe that he is the living God and King of the world. I am astonished and cannot believe this thing. The great and mighty God Whom no eye has seen, Who has neither form nor image, Who said, *For man may not see Me and live* (Exod. 33:20)[22] – how shall I believe that this great inaccessible *Deus absconditus* needlessly entered the womb of a woman, the filthy, foul bowels of a female, compelling the living God to be borm of a woman, a child without knowledge or understanding, senseless, unable to distinguish between his right hand and his left, defecating and urinating, sucking his mother's breasts from hunger and thirst, crying when he is thirsty so that his mother will have compassion on him. Indeed, if she had not suckled him, he would have died of hunger like other

[22] Cf. *Nestor*, p. 9

people. If not, why should she have suckled him? He should have lived miraculously! Why should she have suckled him for nothing, [22b] that he should engage in all foul and miserable human practices?[23] Thus I do not profess this belief which you profess, for my reason does not allow me to diminish the greatness of God, be He exalted, for He has not lessened His glory, be He exalted, nor has He reduced His splendor, be He extolled. If I do not profess this faith which you profess, I am not blameworthy.

I say to you further that if this belief is true, the Creator would not hold me guilty for not believing in His deficiency and the reduction of His grandeur and splendor. *Far be the Lord from evil and the Almighty from injustice!* (Job 34:10) I do not in this respect believe in the diminution of His glory and greatness. If this faith [of theirs] is not true, however, woe to them and to those who believe in it, who diminish the greatness of the high and exalted Lord and who lessen His glorious splendor. I may liken this for you to a human king who changed his garments, shaved his hair, and put on filthy garb and dirty clothes, so that he impaired his noble figure. He then walked alone on the highways without dignity or majesty. Then people came and told someone, "This is the king." If he does not believe [it], the king cannot hold it against him.[24] How much more evident is this with respect to the King of kings, the Holy One, blessed be He. Who would dare to profess this belief which diminishes His greatness, whereby He cannot save His world except by humiliating Himself, debasing His majesty, and befouling His splendor. When mortal kings wish to save the poor of their people, do they not exalt their splendor and increase their glory,

[23] Similar arguments against the incarnation are found in Nestor, pp. 1, 6, 10f.

[24] Similar parables are brought in *Sefer Yosef ha-Meqanne* (ed. Rosenthal), and by Solomon ben Moses de Rossi (Rosenthal, *Meḥqarim,* I, 420).

gather armies and add to their might and majesty? This then is their splendor, and no one can force me to believe this.

The *min* said: How I have listened to your words and contemplated your speech. Pay heed and listen. To lower oneself is the way of humility to teach men humility. [Yet] He [also] performed signs and wonders for He is the Son of God. Because He performed those signs and wonders, I have believed in Him as I and all men are obligated to believe. It was His will to lessen himself and lower himself. As for your parable, know that [23a] of those to whom the king identified himself and showed signs [of his majesty], those who did not do obeisance and homage to him are accountable and those who served him attain greatness.

The *ma'amin* said: Is everyone by whom signs and miracles are performed said to be a God? Were not miracles performed through the agency of the prophets? On this account, do you say that he is God?[25] Now your question concerning the parable is no question, for he who did not serve the king did not sin and he who did not believe that he was a king is not blameworthy ... [What you say] has nothing to do with this, for he who has done homage to a mortal who is not a king is not deserving of death, but he who has worshipped a mortal in place of the living God is deserving of death.

I ask you about the following matters: Was the Divinity which became incarnate in Mary's womb-itself the soul of Jesus, or did he have another soul like other mortals? If you say that he had no soul other than the Divinity which became incarnate, though there was in the flesh a life force other than the Divinity, i.e. the blood which is [also] in beasts and fowl, then the Divinity did not enter a man but an animal.

[25] Cf. *Nestor,* p. 2 and *Yosef ha-Meqanne,* pp. 37-8 which closely resembles the present argument.

Furthermore, since he had no rational soul other than the Divinity, to whom did the Divinity shout when he shouted, *My God, my God, why have you forsaken me* (Ps. 22:2)? How is it that he could not save himself and that he shouted to another? If you say that he had like other mortals a spirit which ascends on high in addition to the Divinity which dwelt in him, then Jesus is like any other man in his body and soul. He is neither God nor the son of God but the Divinity adhered to him. This passed on and his spirit and soul went to Paradise or Gehenna like the souls of the righteous or the wicked. Thus Jesus is neither God nor the son of God by virtue of the Divinity which entered him.[26]

The *min* said: I shall now reprove you and expound my teachings based on the prophecies, some of which are written in the Torah of Moses, some in the prophets, and some in the Writings, most of which originated with David, the man of God. I shall test you and ask you of these [verses] which are all prophecies of Jesus and you shall not be able to contradict or deny any one of them. The first is written in the Book of Genesis: *Let Us make man in Our image, after Our likeness:* then, *and God made man in His image, in the image of God He created him* (Gen. 1:26f.). The plural form of the verb proves [the existence] of the Father, Son, and Spirit as do the plural possessives: *in* Our *image, after* Our *likeness.* In addition, the image and likeness referred to are a human image and likeness which the Divinity adopted in Jesus. You cannot contradict this.

The *ma'amin* said: You have neither teachings nor prophecies which I cannot explain according to their plain sense and context. With reference to the plural form of *Let Us make,*

[26] These characteristic arguments against the concept of the divinity of Jesus were employed by Kimḥi's son David. See *HUCA* XXXVIII (1967), pp. 219f. Cf. *JbR,* pp. 66f.; *Nestor,* p. 5.

some explain that at the beginning of creation, He created the four elements – the higher, fire and air, and the lower, earth and water. Then He gave them the faculty to produce all creatures by virtue of their natural qualities. It is thus written *The earth brought forth vegetation* (v. 12); *let the earth sprout vegetation* (v. 11); *let the earth bring forth swarms* (v. 20). This was so until the sixth day when He created man along with the four elements, saying *Let Us make man.* It is in their nature to produce the body which is material in character, while He breathed into it the supernal soul possessing intellect and rational wisdom.[27] As for image and likeness, nothing which He created in the world resembles Him except man alone. In what does he resemble Him? In the image of dominion and the likeness of rulership, for just as the Holy One, blessed be He, rules over all, so does man rule. It is thus stated *You have given him dominion over Your handiwork. You have put all things under his feet; all sheep and oxen and the beasts of the field, the fowl of the air and the fish of the sea* (Ps. 8:7ff.). This is proven by the text, for after it states, *Let Us make man in Our image, after Our likeness,* it says, *They shall rule the fish of the sea, the birds of the sky* (v. 26). Here image and likeness are not to be taken literally but metaphorically. Image is dominion and likeness is rulership,[28] not a physical image. What is the matter with you? On the basis of one obscure passage, [24a] you deny His unity and

[27] Kimḥi's explanation of the plural forms in Gen. 1:26 is apparently the first known appearance of this interpretation although it is here ascribed to a predecessor. It is cited in his name by his son David and by Naḥmanides in their commentaries *a.l.* Kimḥi may be going back to Midrash Genesis Rabbah 18:3: "*and God said: Let us make man,* etc. With whom did he take counsel? R. Joshua b. Levi said: He took counsel with the works of heaven and earth." See the comm. of Enoch Zundel ben Joseph *(Eẓ Yosef)* on this passage and the comm. of David Kimḥi to Gen. 1:26.

[28] This interpretation of "image" and "likeness" goes back to Saadia Gaon's translation of the Torah *(bi-suratina bi-shibbina musallitan)*. Cf. Ibn Ezra's comm. *a.l.;*

expound it as [proof] of a plurality? Indeed, the philosophers said in their wisdom, "A ship is no good with too many captains," and Solomon said *When a land transgresses, it has too many rulers* (Prov. 28:2).[29] Now if you say that He is more than one, can He act independently or not? If He can act independently, then any addition is superfluous. If not, you believe in an impotent creature. Do you not see that it is apparent from all of creation that there is only one Governor, be He exalted and extolled! I shall explain this with a parable. When we see a book in a uniform hand, we say that one scribe wrote it. Even though it is possible that more than one scribe wrote it, we need not believe this unless there are witnesses to the effect that two or more scribes, whose hands are uniform, wrote it. If reason pointed to less than one scribe, we would believe it. It is clear that the [number of] prior causes is less than the [number of] posterior causes, as is explained in the works of logic, known as the science of *dialectica* and in Arabic as *al-manṭiq*.[30] Now there is one king,

JbR, p. 46.

[29] See Baḥya ibn Paquda, *Duties of the Heart,* 1:7 (ed. Hyamson, p. 38): "Thus Aristotle states in his book in reference to Unity: 'For the transgression of a land, many are the princes thereof' " Cf. *Iliad* II, 204; Arist., *Metaphysics* XII, ch. 10, p. 1076a 4.

[29a] Baḥya ibn Paquda, *Duties of the Heart, ibid.* Saadya Gaon directs a similar argument against the dualists. Cf. *Beliefs and Opinions* II:2, ed. Rosenblatt, pp. 97f.

[30] This argument, interesting in that it reflects the cultural milieu of scribes and scholars, follows Baḥya ibn Paquda, *Duties of the Heart* I:3 (ed. Hyamson, pp. 35f): "We...[ought] not inquire whether He is...more than one or [less than one], since the world could not have come into existence without at least one Creator. If we could possibly conceive that the world could have come into existence with a Creator less than one, we would so conceive Him. But as we cannot conceive that something less than one can bring anything into existence, we conclude that the Creator is One. For in the case of things which are established by adducing proofs, as soon as the existence of those things is proved beyond dispute, we need assume more then is necessary to account for the entire phenomenon, which constitutes the proof. The following will serve as an illustration: When we see a manuscript, uniform in composition and handwriting, it will at once occur to us that one individual wrote and composed it. For it could not conceivably be written by less than one person,

two or three satraps, a number of overseers and officers, and very many soldiers – all under the leadership of the one king. Thus it was with the creation of the world. One Creator stamped all things with their natures and characteristics, so that even though each one functions independently, everything is under the power of the Creator, be He praised. This is similar to the parable of the king and his servants which I mentioned above. Even though each has his own jurisdiction, everything stems from the command of the king.

The *min* said: Tell me. Scripture said that the Creator felt regret and said concerning man *I regret that I made them* (Gen. 6:8). Yet another text says *God is not man to lie, nor the son of man to change,* (Num. 23:19). I ask further: Will the Divinity change His mind and reverse His decision? He said to Jonah the son of Amittai [24b] *In forty days, Nineveh will be overthrown* (Jon. 3:4). Yet it was not overthrown. Therefore, the Creator changed His mind.

The *ma'amin* said: It is true that all this is found in Scripture, but Scripture speaks to those who are intelligent and are capable of understanding it. The fact is that God did not really change His mind, but it is the way of Scripture to speak in ordinary human language. Thus Scripture says, *eyes of God, ears of God, mouth of God, hand of God, face of God, foot of God.* All of this is expressed metaphorically so that people might know something about Him by conceiving of Him as a human being, although the difference between them and Him is great indeed. [This was done] so that the simple might comprehend and understand the Creator, [while] it will not harm the wise, since they will understand the truth of the matter. They will cast away the husks and eat only the fruit. This may be

and if that were possible, we would assume such to be the case. It might indeed have had more than one writer. Still, in the absence of evidence, such as variety of handwriting, etc., we are not warranted in making this assumption."

likened to a man who wishes to water his beast. He will not tell it to drink by speaking to it as he would to another human being but will whistle in accord with its animal nature since it has no intelligence. Similarly did the prophets write of the form of the Creator, so that the simple might understand ... the Creator.[30a] Thus when you see in the Torah that God changed His mind, it is, as we have said, a metaphor used to give the simple some understanding. The fact is that He did not change His mind. Now as for your asking me whether God reverses His decision and as for your bringing a proof from Jonah, I answer: He does not reverse His decision if He says that He will not harm, destroy, or hurt men for their sins. Yet he forgives them and is appeased if they repent. This is an atonement [on their part, on account of which we are] not [to say that] He reversed His decision. Yet one who reverses his decision is one who said he would perform a favor and does not perform that favor without the recipient's having offended him.[31]

The *min* said: What can you say of the passage in the Torah: *The scepter shall not be taken from Judah, nor the ruler (dux) from his thigh until he comes who is to be sent* (Gen. 49:10)? This is Jesus, for when He came, you lost your kingdom

[30a] Baḥya ibn Pakuda, *Duties of the Heart,* ed. Hyamson, pp. 46, 53.

[31] The argument advanced by the *min,* the purpose of which is to provide a basis for the idea that God has changed His inheritance from Judaism to Christianity, is commonly refuted in the writings of the French polemicists. Essentially the same objection and refutation are found in the *Yosef ha-Meqanne* (ed. Rosenthal, p. 37) and the comm. of Joseph Bekhor Shor to Gen. 6:8. See also the *Ḥizzequni* of Ḥizqiah ben Manoaḥ to Gen. 6:6 and the anonymous *Leqeṭ qazar* to the same verse (Cod. Mn. 66, f. 251r). Cf. Midrash Genesis Rabbah 27:4; Rankin, *Jew. Rel. Polemic,* pp. 63f., 71f.
The origin of these arguments requires investigation. They were commonly used against orthodox Christianity by dualist heretics and are frequently refuted in the anti-"Manichaean" texts of the middle ages. See Ebrard of Bethune, *MBVP* XXVI, 1583H; A. Dondaine (ed.), *Liber de duobus principiis* (Rome, 1939), Cf. Augustine, *Civ. Dei.* XVI:11. p. 88. Cf. *JbR,* pp. 25, 34.

and you have neither sovereignty nor king because of what you did to the Messiah.

The *ma'amin* said: Do you not know that this blessing is in the benediction with which Jacob blessed his sons! [25a] He blessed each one of them with his own blessing. In blessing Judah, he gave him the kingship, i.e. the king who would reign over Israel, along with his progeny, would come forth from him. This was David, the first king who ruled over Israel (he and his progeny). This is [the meaning of] *the scepter [shall not depart] from Judah.* From the time that he blessed him, he gave him dominion over his brothers. Thus we have found concerning the [location of the] standards in the desert that it says that the standard of the division of Judah was on the east side[32] and that Moses and Aaron camped near their standard, as it says *Those who were to camp before the Tabernacle, in front – before the Tent of Meeting, on the east – were Moses and Aaron and his sons* (Num. 3:38). *Now the chieftain of the tribe of Judah, Nahshon the son of Aminadab* (Num. 3:2) entered the [red] sea first,[33] for it is written in connection with the war against Canaan *Who will go up for us first against the Canaanites to fight against them? The Lord said: Judah shall go up, for I have delivered the land into his hand* (Jud. 1:1f.). Also in the account [of the events] of Gibeah of Benjamin, Judah was first (Num. 20:18). Therefore, Jacob blessed him, saying that dominion and rulership would not depart from him until David his son comes to receive the kingship. This is [the meaning of] *the scepter shall not depart from Judah, nor the ruler's staff between his feet, until Shiloh comes, and to him shall be the obedience of peoples* (Gen. 49:10). It is known that *shevet* (scepter) and *meḥoqeq* (ruler's staff)

[32] Num. 2:3.
[33] Mekhilta, Beshallaḥ, 5; Midrash Numbers Rabbah 13:7.
[34] Vulgate; *et dux de femore eius.*

represent ranks lower than kingship. Indeed, you translate [*meḥoqeq* by] *duc* and the duke is a governor lower in rank than the king. This was [the status of] Nahshon the chieftain and the chieftains after him until David came. They continued to be rulers over the rest of the tribes until David, who received the kingship, was born. This may be likened to a king who deigned to grant a patent of nobility to one of his servants for a limited period. In the interim, until the termination of that period, he says, "You shall have authority and this province shall be under your jurisdiction." Thus Judah was told that dominion would not pass from his sons until David came to receive his kingship.

How can you! Do you not see the prophecies? For more than four hundred years before the coming of Jesus, the kingship had passed from the house of David. The last king from the house [25b] of David was Zedekiah whom Nebuchadnezzar king of Babylon blinded and led into exile. After him there arose no king from the House of David, for all the kings in the time of the Second Temple were priests. Likewise Herod was a slave and also was not of the House of David. Now the number of years from the Babylonian exile, until the [destruction of the] Second Temple, was four hundred and twenty, and Jesus lived towards [the time of] the destruction of the Second Temple when Jerusalem was destroyed. How then can you say that the kingship of the House of David did not pass until Jesus came. I shall show that it had passed four hundred and twenty years before the coming of Jesus. Your words are false and your belief is untrue. This is clear and evident.[35]

[35] See introduction,. The above section was published by A. Posnanski in *Schiloh* (Leipzig, 1904), German, pp. 139f.; Hebrew, pp. XIXf. Kimḥi's interpretation is in accord with Ibn Ezra *(Schiloh,* pp. 108ff.). See especially the commentary of David Kimḥi to Gen. 49:10 and Rosenthal, *Meḥqarim,* I, 402.

The *min* said: I shall show you clearly that Moses ... prophesied concerning Jesus, for he said: *The Lord your God will raise up for you a prophet from among your brethren like myself; him you shall heed* (Dt. 18:16). Of this Scripture said: *If anybody fails to hear the words he speaks in My name, I Myself will call him to account* (ibid., v. 19). Now you have not heeded His words but have denied Him and are in exile among the nations from that time on for *this is the reckoning for his blood.* (Gen. 42:22).

The *ma'amin* said: Was Jesus then a prophet? Did you not say at first that he was the son of God? If he is the one about whom Moses prophesied, then Moses was greater than he, for the Torah had borne witness concerning him that *never again did there arise in Israel a prophet like Moses, whom the Lord singled out,* etc. (Dt. 34:10). Now if you say that [the intention of the verse is that] no one arose in [Moses'] own time but that one did arise at a later time, what is so exceptional about Moses? No other prophets had yet appeared, for Isaiah, Jeremiah, Ezekiel, and all the other prophets came later. Also, Scripture says *in Israel like Moses.* If you say, "Why did it say, *there did not arise* instead of *there shall not arise?*", know that in many places prophecies are written according to the way they will be read at a future date. It says *there did not arise* in accordance with the way it would be read forever and for all eternity. In every age, they will read it *there did not arise.*[36]

The *min* said: You understand most of the Torah literally[37]

[36] This text was first applied to Jesus in Acts 3:22f. The Christological interpretation of this verse is refuted also in *JbR*, pp. 59f. with a somewhat different approach. Cf. also Saadia, *Beliefs and Opinions,* II:6; *Yosef ha-Meqanne,* ed. Rosenthal, p. 61. On the Muslim interpretation of this passage, see S. Baron, *Soc. and Rel. Hist. of the Jews* (Philadelphia, 1957), V, 87; M. Perlman (ed.), *'Ifḥām el-Yahūd, PAAJR* XXXII (1964), p. 45.

[37] In the Hebrew: *pyltr',* probably *ped de la letra,* cf. *au pied de la lettre.*

[26a] while we understand if figuratively. Your whole reading of the Bible is erroneous for you resemble him who gnaws at the bone, while we [suck at] the marrow within. You are like the beast that eats the chaff, while we [eat] the wheat.[38]

The *ma'amin* said: Tell me. When the Holy One, blessed be He, gave the Torah to Moses who taught it to Israel, did he understand it figuratively or not? If you say that he did not understand it figuratively but literally and taught it so to Israel, then Israel is not to be held accountable in this matter. How is it that the Creator did not teach it to Moses figuratively so that he might have taught it [so] to Israel? If you say that he understood it figuratively, why did he not teach it to Israel figuratively? For that matter, why did the prophets who came after him not do so? Indeed the prophets understood [the laws] according to the intention of Moses. Joshua circumcised the people and celebrated the Passover, as did Hezekiah and Josiah, according to the command of Moses. It was so with other commandments. What will you say of the Sabbath? Did Moses not try the one who gathered sticks [on the Sabbath] and did not Ezra exhort the people concerning the Sabbath? Further, if the cessation of [immoral] activities is not dependent on the seventh day since they are forbidden the entire week, why did the Torah not teach it allegorically as you say?[39]

Know that the fact is that the Torah is not [to be taken] altogether literally or altogether figuratively. If one says to his servant, "Take the horse and ride it on the sea," we must try to interpret this figuratively; likewise, if he says to him,

[38] Cf. Rosenthal, *Meḥqarim,* II, 444; *Yosef ha-Meqanne,* p. xxvii; *AJ,* pp. 19, 21, 164; cf. Ambrose, *Lib. de Paradiso,* 65f.; *PL* XIV, 325.

[39] This argument refutes the Christian teaching that the Sabbath is a moral commandment prohibiting the performance of evil deeds and applies to no one particular day. See AJ, pp. 272, 291, 303; *DTC,* IV, pt. 1, 1308f.

"Board the ship and go in it on dry land." There is no need for figurative interpretation if he says to him, "Board the ship and go on the sea in it." Some commandments may be understood both literally and figuratively. *Circumcise yourselves to the Lord and take away the foreskins of your heart* (Jer. 4:4) is to be taken figuratively, but *at the age of eight days, every male among you shall be circumcised* (Gen. 17:12) is to be taken literally. Both the circumcision of the flesh, i.e. the flesh of the foreskin and of the heart are obligatory, [26b] (i.e. we must circumcise our flesh and our hearts.)[40] The prophet Ezekiel said *No uncircumcised in heart nor uncircumcised in flesh shall enter My sanctuary* (Ezek. 44:9). Now you are uncircumcised in flesh – which you cannot deny. If you are prevented from [entering] His sanctuary on one count, you are most certainly prevented [from doing so] on two. Now you cannot claim that you are not uncircumcised in heart, for whoever transgresses the commandments and murders, fornicates, steals, oppresses, speaks abusively to people, and mocks and robs them is uncircumcised in heart. You are uncircumcised in heart and uncircumcised in flesh while Israel are circumcised in heart and circumcised in flesh. You will not find a Jew who has been hanged or who has had his eyes gouged or who has had one of his limbs cut off on account of crimes he has committed. Now if you say that the Torah was [to be understood] literally but that Jesus came afterward and commanded us a law of grace and explained it figuratively and introduced baptism, known as *batisme,* instead of circumcision and Sunday instead of the Sabbath, then the Creator changed His mind, for He gave the Torah for a limited time only.

[40] The above passage from Jeremiah was frequently brought as a proof that circumcision was to be understood figuratively and not literally. See *AJ,* pp. 46, 302.; *Yosef ha-Meqanne,* ed. Rosenthal, p. 72.

Is it not said *This is My covenant with them, says the Lord, My spirit that is upon you and My words which I have put in your mouth will not depart from mouth* (Isa. 59:21). How can we say that He would change this Torah which he said would never depart from our mouths?[41]

The *min* said: Daniel said *When the Most Holy comes, your anointing shall cease.*[42] This refers to Jesus, for when Jesus came, your dominion and Messiah were lost.

The *ma'amin* said: See how you are wrong on several counts. Firstly, in the Book of Daniel there is no verse such as you have quoted *when the Most Holy comes, your anointing shall cease.* Scripture says *to anoint the most holy* (Dan. 9:24) and in another place *the anointed one shall be cut off and be no more* (v. 24). You do not understand this passage. At the beginning of the passage, it says *Seventy weeks are decreed upon your people and upon your holy city, to finish the transgression and to make an end of sin, and to forgive iniquity, and to bring in everlasting righteousness, and to seal vision* [27a] *and prophet, and to anoint the most holy* (v. 24). Afterwards, it says: *Know therefore and discern that from the going forth of the word to restore and build Jerusalem unto one anointed, a prince, shall be seven weeks; and for sixty-two weeks it shall be built again with broad place and moat, but in troublous times.* (v. 25). Then it says *After the sixty-two weeks an anointed one will be cut off and be no more; and the people of a prince that shall come shall destroy the sanctuary; but his end shall be with a flood; and unto the end of the war*

[41] See *HUCA* XXXVIII (1967), 218ff.

[42] This reading goes back to a sixth century text wrongly ascribed to Augustine: "cum venerit sanctus cessabit unctio vestra." See E. N. Stone, "A Translation...of the pseudo-Augustinian Sermon...concerning the Creed", *Univ. of Wash. Publ. in Lang. and Lit.*, IV (1928), 201; "A Religious Play of the Twelfth Century", *Univ. of Wash. Publ. in Lang. and Lit.*, IV (1926), 189; *AJ*, p. 323. It is discussed in the *Sefer Nizzahon Yashan*, Jacob ben Reuben, Solomon ben Moses de Rossi, and Moses of Salerno. See *JbR*, pp. 135ff; Rosenthal, *Meḥqarim*, I, 407; Rankin, *Jew. Rel. Polemic*, pp. 55f., 68, 136f.; Posnanski, *Schiloh*, Heb. p. XXIV.

desolations are determined (v. 26). If you know how to explain this passage, I shall listen to what you have to say. Yet if you do not know how to explain it, be still and listen to me, and I shall teach you wisdom. Daniel said *I pondered the books, over the number of years, whereof the word of the Lord came to Jeremiah the prophet, that He would accomplish for the desolation of Jerusalem seventy years* (v. 2). Now I ask you what these, concerning which he said *I pondered the books,* were. If you can, answer me, and if not, hear me out. These books were the *Sefer ha-galui* and the *Sefer ha-miqneh* which the prophet Jeremiah acquired from his uncle along with the field.[43] Concerning these he was commanded *Take these books,* etc. (Jer. 32:14) and it is written *And put them in an earthen vessel that they may last a long time (ibid.).* He studied those books and saw that they were fulfilled and then he fasted. Then the angel came and said: *or from the first day that you began to understand and fast before God, your words were heard and I came because of your words* (Dan. 10:12). The angel came to reveal to him the mysterious prophecies and stated explicitly *Seventy weeks, etc.* These seventy weeks are seventy weeks of years, *viz.* four hundred and ninety years – seventy of the Babylonian exile and four hundred and twenty years of the existence of the second Temple.[44] These figures are well known. Now he divided this period and said that from the beginning of the period ..., *from the going forth of the word to restore and rebuild Jerusalem unto one anointed, a prince, shall be seven weeks, and for sixty-two weeks, it shall be built again with broad place and moat and in troublous times* (Dan. 9:25). *Unto one anointed, a prince* refers to Cyrus[45] of whom it is said *To His anointed,*

[43] Jer. 32:12ff., cited by David Kimḥi, *Shorashim, s.v. spr.*

[44] Babylonian Talmud, Yoma 91; Rashi on Dan. 9:24; *Sefer ha-Galui* (ed. Mathews), p. 54.

[45] See Rashi a.l.

to Cyrus, whose right hand I have held (Isa. 45:1) and of whom it is said *He shall build My city and set free My exiles, not for price* [27b] *nor reward* (*ibid.*, v. 13). The sixty two weeks were from the time they left Babylon to the time when the anointed one was cut off, as it is said *And after the sixty-two weeks shall an anointed one be cut off and be no more.* Now the phrase, *your anointed one shall be cut off,* which you cited is not in the book. The truth is that this anointed one of yours is king Agrippa[46] whom the wicked Titus killed, for in his days Jerusalem and the Temple, may it be rebuilt speedily and in our days, were destroyed. The phrase *and be no more* means that he has no one to replace him,[47] for no king of Israel rose after him until this day. Now there is one week remaining from the figure of seventy weeks, for first he counted seven weeks and then sixty-two making sixty-nine. Afterwards he said *He shall make a firm covenant with many for one week* (Dan. 9:27), thereby making seventy weeks. One of the commentators said that the half week [of which it is said], *And for half a week he shall cause the sacrifice and offering to cease (ibid.)* is part of that week of which he said that he would make a firm covenant with many for one week. That half week is three and a half years.[48] I have thus clarified your first error.

Now as for your second error according to which you said that [the expression] "most holy" could refer only to God. With reference to the altar, does it not say *The altar shall become most holy* (Exod. 29:37, 40:10). So was all the apparatus of the Temple which was anointed with the anointing oil most holy.[49] The meaning of *decreed upon your people and upon*

[46] See Rashi to Dan. 9:26; *Sefer ha-Galui,* p. 54.

[47] The text reads: *'en lo maqom.* The translation is in accord with the text found in Kimḥi's *Sefer ha-Galui,* p. 54.

[48] See Rashi to Dan. 9:27; *Sefer ha-Galui,* p. 54.

[49] Exod. 30:29.

your holy city is this: It says: *Seventy weeks are decreed upon your people, etc.* until the sixty weeks in Jerusalem are completed.[50] After this it was decreed that they be exiled and remain in exile for a long period *to finish the transgression, and to make an end of sin, and to forgive iniquity.* By the weight of their afflictions, their transgression would be finished, their sins would be made an end of, and their iniquity would be forgiven.[51] Afterwards, He would bring everlasting righteousness, of which David said, *Truth springs out of the earth and righteousness springs down from heaven* (Ps. 85:12). This refers to Messiah, the son of David, for whom we hope and of whom it is said *to anoint the most holy.* In his days, there would appear everlasting righteousness [28a] which would never turn into deceit. How deceitful is the world [as it is, made up] of gentiles *(goyim),* and Ishmaelites, and Jews. At that time, however, there will be fulfilled *For then I will turn to the peoples a pure language ... to serve Him with one consent* (Zeph. 3:9). Then will there be everlasting righteousness. The meaning of *to seal vision and prophet* is that then every vision and prophet will be completely fulfilled, for the words of the prophests [consist of] nothing [but] chastisement [or] consolation.[52] Thus all of the words of the prophets will be fulfilled as it is said in the psalm of Solomon. *Give the king your judgments, O God, and Your righteousness to the king's son* (Ps. 72:1), which he concluded with *the prayers of David, the son of Jesse, are ended* (*ibid.,* v. 20), for his prayers will no longer be said. How will they say, "save us," when they are saved; "deliver us," when they are already delivered; "forgive our sins", when He has already said *You will be clean from*

[50] until the destruction of the Temple.

[51] See Rashi a.l.

[52] The text reads: *ki 'en be-divre ha-nevi'im pur'anut u-neḥamah.* Perhaps the intent of the author is to say that Scripture contains more than what is found in the sum of its details alone.

all your your uncleanness and I will cleanse you from your idols (Ezek. 36:25). Then will they acknowledge and bless the name of our God. Of this he said *to seal vision and prophet and to anoint the most holy.*

The *min* said: *All things are difficult*[53] (Eccl. 1:8), but I shall ask concerning one passage in Isaiah. You will not be able to deny that it prophesied concerning Jesus and concerning Mary. [I refer to] that which he said *A virgin shall conceive and bear a son and shall call his name Immanuel* (Isa. 7:14). Now no virgin in the world except Mary ever gave birth and [since] Jesus is the son of God, she called his name Immanuel (God is with us).

(The sage, R. Isaac Halevi [54] of blessed memory replied: I agree with your saying, *the virgin shall conceive and bear a son,* for there are found many such women. There are many former virgins who have been found pregnant, but when they are pregnant, they are not virgins, and when they are virgins, they are not pregnant. It is as if one were to say, "This vineyard shall be a field." It is not a vineyard when it is a field and if it is a vineyard it is not a field. Similarly, if it says *a virgin shall conceive,* it is so, However, [28b] once she has conceived, she is not a virgin.)

The *ma'amin* said: I have been putting up with your questions and answering them steadily but I have not yet asked about your [interpretations of the] prophecies. Stop then and let me begin with my questions so that you may answer them. [Before doing so,] however, I shall say a few words concerning the way in which those who have explained this passage have strayed from the path of reason. They did not perceive clearly that the passage to which you referred is not in Scripture.

[53] After the Vulgate: Cunctae res difficiles.

[54] See introduction,

Rather, Jerome your translator is the one who led you astray and caused you to err. *May he rest in the congregation of the shades* (Prov. 21:16). You said, *the virgin shall conceive,* but Scripture says the *young woman shall conceive.* Now *'almah* means "young woman," be she a virgin or not. [She may be a] virgin [as in the verse], *Let the young woman who comes out to draw* ... (Gen. 24:43) or not, [as in] *the way of a man with a young woman* (Prov. 30:19). Similarly, a young man may be called an *'elem,* as it is said of David, *Whose son is this* 'elem (I Sam. 17:56)?, as if to say, "Whose son is this young man?" This is all false, for it is not found so in the Book of Origen,[55] the most ancient and authoritative [text and the one] from which your text was translated. Everything is dependent upon it for it was dictated by the prophets, and Jerome the translator relied upon it, translated from it, and trusted it, with the exception of a few words which he did not understand or which were contrary to his belief and which he altered, changing the root of the faith to wormwood.[56]

Furthermore, if, according to your interpretation, she were a virgin giving birth, how can one believe that this is a sign? Would not people suspect that she played the harlot and this child was illegitimate? In addition, what sort of sign would this be for Ahaz, king of Judah, concerning his troubles with those kings who attacked him – the king of Samaria, Pekah, the son of Remaliah, and Rezin, the king of Aram. Now Scripture said *His heart and the heart of his people were moved as the trees of the forest are moved with the wind* (Isa. 7:2). At that time, the Holy One, blessed be He, said to Isaiah *Go forth to meet Ahaz ... and say to him: Keep calm and be quiet; do not fear nor let your heart be faint because of*

[55] See introduction,
[56] See introduction,

these two tails of smoking firebrands (*ibid.*, vv. 3f.). Afterwards, the prophet said to Ahaz *Ask a sign of the Lord, your God; ask it in the depth or in the height above* (v. 11), [29a] [i.e.] in the heavens or the earth below. Ahaz answered *I will not ask nor will I try the Lord* (v. 12). Now his intention was evil for he did not believe that the Creator could give him a sign.[57] The prophet then said to him, *Hear now, O house of David. Is it a small thing for you to weary my God also? Therefore, the Lord Himself will give you a sign. The young woman shall conceive a son and shall call his name Immanuel* (vv. 13f.). Now it was quite clear and evident that this sign was [given] to Ahaz in order to give him some encouragement. Now if this sign referred to Jesus, as you say, what sort of sign was it for Ahaz who never saw him and in whose time he did not live? Let it be known to you that nothing which comes after the event is ever called a sign. If the event has already taken place, the event is already known, and what need is there for the sign? Rather, the sign comes before the event so that people will know for certain, when they see the sign, that the event will take place. The sign should then properly be before the event as we found in the case of King Hezekiah. When he became ill, he said, *What is the sign that I shall go up to the House of the Lord, etc.* (Isa. 38:22)?, and the sign came before the event. Similarly Gideon asked for a sign with the fleece of wool and said, *If there be dew upon the fleece only and it be dry upon all the ground* (Jud. 6:37). On the second day, he asked the opposite and said, *Let it now be dry only upon the fleece, and upon all the ground, let there be dew* (ibid. v. 39). Thus the sign came before the event. Further, as I told you, nothing is called a sign or a portent which [appears] dubious to people, such as this sign. To say that a virgin will give birth [would seem] dubious to people, for they will not believe that she did not play the harlot. That which is called a sign is that which cannot be imitated, doubted, or foretold. We have seen many young women who were considered virgins but gave birth. Then we knew for a certainty that they were not virgins.[58]

Now [even] if you say that we must believe that he was the Messiah, son of a virgin, because he performed miracles and wonders, we need not believe that he was the son of God because of the wonders. Further, if [29b] you say that he revived the dead, Elijah and his disciples revived the dead and they were not God. Further, Scripture said that God would give Ahaz this sign as it is said, *The Lord Himself shall give you a sign.*

The *min* said: If so, who was this Immanuel and what was the sign that He gave to Ahaz? I do not see that a male child, Immanuel, was born to him.

The *ma'amin* said: I shall tell you who Immanuel was and what the sign and portent was. Immanuel was the son of King Ahaz.[59] He called his name Immanuel because from the day that this young man was to be born, God would be with them.[60] Up to that time, God was not with them nor did He help them. Pekah the son of Remaliah had captured them, exiled [the inhabitants of] his land, and killed all his soldiers. It states in Chronicles that in one battle he killed two hundred thousand from among his forces.[61] In his time, there was

[58] This material, dealing with the "corruption" of Isa. 7:14 and that which follows, is restated in the *Sefer ha-Galui,* pp. 134ff. and is cited by David Kimḥi in his commentary and in the *Shorashim, s.v. 'lm. JbR* is much briefer on this point. See p. 84. Cf. Blumenkranz, *TZ* IV (1948), 135; Hailprin, *Rashi,* pp. 164ff.

[59] This rather unusual identification of Immanuel is cited as an anonymous interpretation in Ibn Ezra.

[60] Immanuel in Hebrews means "God is with us."

[61] II Chron. 28:6. The figure stated in the text is one hundred and twenty thousand.

fulfilled *Seven women shall take hold of one man on that day and say, "We will eat our own bread and wear our own clothing; only let us be called by your name, take away our shame"* (Isa. 4:1), for the warriors were killed with very few remaining. Now Hezekiah was the son of Ahaz and ruled after him. Of this it is said *A child is born to us, a son is given to us.* This is in reference to Hezekiah. When Immanuel was born, God gave them a sign through him that He would be with them and that these kings would do them no harm. Now if you ask what this sign was, I shall tell you that the sign was [the following]. He told him, *The young woman shall conceive and bear a son,* for the wife of Ahaz was pregnant. Then when she bears the son, his name will be called Immanuel. This is the sign: *Curd and honey shall he eat, when he knows to refuse the evil and choose the good* (7:15), for as soon as he is born, he will choose the good and refuse the evil and know that he should eat curds and honey. It is a great sign that a tiny infant should distinguish between good and evil as soon as he is born.[62]

The *min* said: You said that a sign comes only before the event, [but] this took place after the event. It already said, *Before the child shall know to refuse the evil and choose the good, the land ... of which you have a horror shall be forsaken* (7:16). Thus He said that the land would be forsaken [30a] first and that the sign would appear afterwards.

The *ma'amin* said: When you know what the event [actually] is, then you will know whether the sign came before the event or after the event. Know that the event is this. Know that Ahaz was afraid because the two kings said, *Let us go up against Judah and disquiet it. Let us make a breach in it for us and set up a king, the son of Tabeel, in it* (Isa. 7:6). Their intention was to go up to Jerusalem and conquer it, to dethrone the

[62] Kimḥi's interpretation of the sign is similar to that of Ibn Ezra.

House of David, and to set up one of their own as king. Of this the prophet said, *It shall not be fulfilled nor shall it come to pass, for the head of Aram is Damascus, etc. ..., and the head of Samariah is Remaliah's son* (*ibid.*, vv. 7ff.) – and they shall not be heads. The prophet then gave him a sign that their plan would never be realized. It is this which is the event. The event is not the fact that they would leave Jerusalem, for if they left Jerusalem once, they might come back a second time. Rather, when Ahaz sees this sign, he will be encouraged [in the conviction] that the kings of Israel would never conquer Jerusalem as he feared. The verse, *Before the child shall know to refuse the evil and choose the good, the land of whose two kings you have a horror shall be abandoned*, refers to the fact that they will not be afraid that they will besiege him, for they will depart from him before the sign. When Ahaz sees this, he will be encouraged [to believe] that they will not conquer Jerusalem. This is [the meaning of his] saying, *of whose two kings you have a horror.* Their plan [to be Judah's two kings] is [only] wishful thinking on their part. This will not be carried out.[63] I have now explained and clarified your problems so that you have nothing left to say in this matter. I have shown that interpretation of this passage in reference to Jesus and Mary is problematic and untenable.

The *min* said: I shall ask another question. In Psalm [110] it says, *The Lord said to my Lord, Sit at My right hand, until I make Your enemies Your footstool* (v. 1).

The *ma'amin* said: Jerome your translator has corrupted the text by saying, *The Lord said to my Lord ('adonai)*. In our text, the most authoritative, it is written, *The Lord said to my lord ('adoni)*. The vowel sign is *ḥiriq* [indicating a reading of

[63] See above, n. 58. Kimḥi's exegesis of Isa. 7:16 according to which "the land" refers to Judah appears to be original. See comm. of David Kimḥi a.l.

'adoni] and not *pataḥ* [calling for a reading of *'adonai* (Lord)] as you said.[64] Therefore, [30b] the meaning is not properly understood by you. Further, he translated *Your people offer themselves willingly* (v. 3) as *Yours is the princeship.*[65] The poet who composed this psalm did so in reference to David, as it is said, *A psalm concerning David (le-David). The Lord said to my lord,* etc. The [preposition] *lamed* of *le-David* is like the *lamed* of [the phrase] *le-'avadim ve-li-shefaḥot* (Deut. 28:68), [i.e.] *with respect to being male and female slaves.*[66] (Now Rabbi Moses of blessed memory said that even though David composed the psalms through the holy spirit, only the Levites were entitled to sing them as is mentioned in Chronicles.[67] Now David composed this psalm, and the psalm [beginning] *The Lord will answer you on the day of sorrow* (Ps. 20), and the psalm [beginning] *O Lord, in Your power the king will rejoice* (Ps. 21) in [third person] in such a way that when the Levite sang it, the audience would understand that it refers to David.)[68] The entire psalm, *The Lord said to my lord* through *until I make your enemies your footstool,* was [composed] at the beginning of his reign. When the Phillistines heard that Israel had anointed David as king, they came to fight with him.[69]

[64] The Vulgate translates "Dixit Dominus Domino meo". The capitalized "Domino" indicates that the "Lord" here is understood as divine, as if the Hebrew read "'adonai". The masoretic text reads "'adoni", "my lord." While David Kimḥi remarks in his commentary a.l. "that they read it with a *qamaẓ* on the *nun*", R. Joseph ascribes a reading with a *pataḥ* to the Christians. On this whole problem, see U. Simon, *"RaBa' we-RaDaQ – shte gishot li-she'elat mehemanut nusaḥ ha-miqra"*, *Shenaton Bar-Ilan,* VI (1967-8), 210ff., 220ff.

[65] *Tecum principium* of the Vulgate presumably presupposes *'imkha nedivut* instead of *'amkha nedavot* of the Masoretic Text. See David Kimḥi, *Comm.* to Ps. 110, end.

[66] This interpretation is cited by David Kimḥi although a different proof text is brought. On this use of the *lamed,* see the comm. to Psalms of David Kimḥi, introd. and Ps. 20:1. *JbR* brings interpretation similar to that of Joseph Kimḥi but does not deal with the textual question. See also *Nestor,* p. 5; *HUCA* XXXVIII (1967), 216.

[67] I Chron. 15:2, 16ff.

[68] See introduction,

[69] Cited by David Kimḥi a.l.

[God] said that He would go forth before him to fight with them, as it is said, *When you hear the sound of marching in the tops of the mulberry trees, bestir yourself.* (II Sam. 5:24). It says too, *David came to Baal-perazim and David defeated them there* (*ibid.*, v. 20). *The Lord at your right hand crushes kings in the day of his wrath* (Ps. 110:5), for he wreaked vengeance on the Phillistines and the other nations through David, as it is said, *David hamstrung all the chariot horses but left enough for a hundred chariots* (II Sam. 8:4, I Chron. 18:4).

Now how does the sitting at [God's] right hand apply to Jesus? How could He say [referring to him], *Sit at My right hand until I make your enemies your footstool* and *The Lord sends forth from Zion your mighty scepter. Rule in the midst of your foes* (v. 2). If this was said with reference to Jesus, why must He send forth his might from Zion? He is the son of God, in your opinion, and God should maintain Himself without the help of His Father.[70]

The *min* said: This is made evident in [Psalm 72], *Of Solomon, Give the king Your judgment, O God, and Your justice to the son of the king.* It is evident that Jesus is the son of the King and that the entire psalm was said with reference to Him. There are things in the psalm which cannot possibly [31a] be explained with reference to a human being. How can you explain, *May he be like rain that falls on the mown grass* (v. 6)?

The *ma'amin* said: In this psalm, more than three [personages are mentioned]: Solomon, God, the king, the son of the king, and the singer of the Psalm ...,[71] i.e. five.[72] I shall

[70] See David Kimḥi, end Ps. 110, ed. Bosniak, pp. 66f.

[71] Heb. unclear.

[72] Cf. comm. of David Kimḥi to Ps. 72, end (ed. Esterson, *HUCA* X (1935), 442f.): "You may refute their words by telling them: You say that the Trinity is [represented] in this verse [by the words] "God", "King", and "king's son." Now you say that "Solomon" refers to the Divinity. If so, there are four." Cf. Petrus Alfonsi, *Dialogus, PL* CLVII, 622; Jerome, *Brev. in Ps., PL* XXVI, 1027.

explain that which is difficult for you. *May he be like rain that falls on the mown grass* means the [following]. Just as the rain falls on the new mown grass so that the world be rich and fertile, so may the righteous be in his days. It is so written afterwards, *In his days may the righteous flourish and peace abound till the moon be no more* (v. 7). How can you interpret this with reference to Jesus? It says in the psalm, *May all kings fall down to him, all nations serve him* (v. 11). Now we have seen that all kings did not fall down before him nor did all nations serve him. The Ishmaelites and the Jews have not served him but have denied him.[72a] In addition, it says in the psalm, *May he have dominion from sea to sea and from the River to the ends of the earth* (v. 8). Does not the Creator, be He exalted, rule over the whole universe? His dominion is over the heavens and the earth, land and sea.[73] He needs no boundaries in His domain for the entire earth is under His rule. May God in His righteousness save us from such a belief. May His people Israel, His own people, not stumble into belief in a ruler whose rule is limited in extent. *Blessed be God in His domain – the God of Israel Who alone does wonders. Amen. Blessed be His glorious name for ever and ever. May His glory fill the whole earth. Amen and Amen.* (vv. 18f.)

The *min* said: I shall show you [evidence] of the Trinity in the Torah of Moses which you will not be able to refute. When Abraham was circumcised, God appeared to him as it is said, *The Lord appeared to him by the plains of Mamre; sitting ..., etc. When he looked up, there appeared three men standing near him.* (Gen. 18:1f.) At first he saw one but he prayed to

[72a] *Yosef ha-meqanne*, ed. Rosenthal, p. 121.

[73] Cf. *Comm.* of David Kimḥi a.l.: "If this [refers] to the Divinity, there is no bound in His dominion. His dominion is over the entire universe, heaven and earth." *JbR* (p. 74) refutes the Christological interpretation of Ps. 72 but in a different fashion. Cf. *Disputation* of Naḥmanides in Rankin, *Jew. Rel. Polemic*, p. 192.

three. When he first saw the one, he said, *Lord, if I have found favor in your sight, do not go on past your servant* (v. 3). Afterwards, he said, *Let me bring water and bathe your feet* [31b] *and recline under the tree. And let me fetch a morsel of bread, etc.* (vv. 4f.). They stood by him and he gave them food and drink. They appeared to eat and drink. Now at first he spoke in the singular and afterwards he saw three and spoke in the plural. These [three] are the Father, the Son, and the Holy Spirit.[74]

The *ma'amin* said: *Suffer me a little and I will tell you* (Job 36:2). I shall demonstrate to you your foolishness in this passage, The first statement, *the Lord appeard to him,* refers to the fact that the Holy One, blessed be He, revealed Himself to Abraham to disclose to him the destruction of Sodom and Gomorrah. We have thus found that after the three men went, the Holy One, blessed be He, appeared to him, as it is said, *Now the Lord had said, Shall I hide from Abraham what I am about to do* (v. 17)? Now this entire section as it is written refers to [God's] revelation to him in reference to the destruction of Sodom, in accordance with the saying of the prophet, *The Lord God will do nothing without revealing His counsel to His servants the prophets* (Amos 3:7). Why God revealed Himself to him is then evident. There is [another] reason for this, [namely,] to heal him from the circumcision. *Looking up, he saw* means that when he was with the Holy One, blessed be He, he looked up and saw three men. If it is as you say, what is the point of *Looking up, he saw?* It should have said, *The Lord appeared to him, and he looked very carefully, and there were three men.* Rather, it says, *looking up, he saw,* which means that he looked over to another place after God appeared to him. Now your reference to his seeing one and praying to

[74] On this verse in religious polemics, see Baron, *History* V, 121.

three is not in the text at all. It does say, *As soon as he saw them, he ran from the entrance of the tent to greet them and bowing down,...* (v. 2). Now bowing is not praying, for bowing is said in reference [to showing homage] to human beings. It is said, *Then Abraham bowed low before the people of the land* (Gen. 23:12).

You will find that these three were emissaries from God for three [different] purposes. One [came] to inform Sarah as it is said, *I will return to you when life is due, and your wife Sarah shall have a son* (18:10). The [other] two went to Sodom, one to save Lot and the other to destroy Sodom. Now the three of them were angelic emissaries. If you say that they were the Creator, then He became incarnate before the advent of Jesus who is the Son. Now Jesus, who is the Son, became incarnate, and in this instance all three, the Father, the Son, and the Spirit, became incarnate, for they appeared in the form [32a] of men.

He spoke at first in the singular, *If it please you,* because he was addressing the most prominent one among them, for it is customary to address the member of a group who appears the most prominent when one wishes to offer them hospitality.

This is what he did and he said, *Do not go on past your servant. Let a little water be brought.* [It is as if one] were to say, "Please stop over with me, [you] and your friends, and I shall prepare food for you." Now if, as you say, the Creator appeared to him in the form of three men, how did He change back into one when the [other] two went off to Lot in Sodom, as the verse says, *The men went on from there to Sodom, while Abraham remained standing before the Lord* (Gen. 18:22). Tell me also: Which one separated himself from the other two, the Father, the Son, or the Spirit? What about the one that became separated? Why did the Creator appear to Lot in the form of two men and to Abraham as three? Indeed, he who believes in two [deities] will not go wrong with your theory for two appeared to Lot. God save us from this faith and anything resembling it![75]

The *min* said: It states quite explicitly in the psalter that the Creator who is supreme was born, for the Creator said, *I will make mention of Rahab and Babylon, them that know Me. Behold Aliens, and Tyre, and the people of Ethiopia; this one was there. But to Zion a man shall say: A man was born in her, and the Most High Himself established her* (Ps. 87:4f.).[76]

The *ma'amin* said: See how your first words contradict your faith, for it says, *I will mention Rahab and Babylon.* In the future, Israel will mention those places where they were exiled: Egypt and Babylon, for Rahab is Egypt,[77] *and Philistia and Tyre, with Ethiopia.* They will look at those who were born in those lands while in exile and say, *This one was born there,* for they will not be as big as those born in Zion. *This one was born there* is said by way of deprecation. *And of Zion it shall be said, This man and that man were born in her;* the expression, *this man and that man,* [refers to the fact that] they were all choice individuals, mighty men of renown. *For* [32b] *the Most High Himself will establish her;* i.e. Zion. It says of God that He will establish her. Now if you say, "How may *'elyon* be said of a human being?", why are you surprised at this?[78] Does it not say of Israel, *He will set you high ('elyon)* above all the nations (Deut. 26:19) and of the Temple which

[75] Joseph Kimḥi's solution to the problem, based on the rabbinic interpretation in Babylonian Talmud, Bava Meẓi'a 89b, is found in a less developed form in *JbR,* pp. 64f. and in *Yosef ha-Meqanne,* ed. Rosenthal, p. 39.

[76] Jerome apparently read the verb in the active, *"yomar",* rather than in the passive, *"ye'amer",* as in the Masoretic Text: "Numquid Sion dicet homo: 'et homo natus in ea' ", the "homo natus" being Jesus. See *PL* XXVI, 1085. The refutation here is that more one person is mentioned as being born and not one alone.

[77] Cf. Isa. 30:7.

[78] Jewish interpretation tended to refer *'elyon* to Jerusalem rather than to God. See Rashi, Menaḥem ha-Meiri, a.l.; *JbR,* p. 75; *Yosef ha-Meqanne,* p. 113. The material in this paragraph is found in the comm. of David Kimḥi, Ps. 87, end.

is mere wood and stone, and *this house which is so high* (I Kings 9:8). You will find also, *the upper gate of the House of the Lord* (II Kings 15:35, II Chron. 27:3) along with many usages of *'elyon* which do not apply to the Creator including the present instance. There is no need for this. I answer: The meaning is that those born in other lands do not resemble those born in Zion and the Creator will establish her for He is Most High. Would that you could clearly demonstrate to me that which Jesus made sound in Jerusalem, for it never bereaved its inhabitants of children as much as [it did] after him [up through] today.

In this vein, Ezekiel said, *And no longer bereave your nation of children* (Ezek. 36:14). Indeed most of those who travel there become seriously ill and afterwards Ishmaelites seize them from the hands of the gentiles.[79] This is not *He will establish her* but *He will destroy her.*

Now you may say that he did not [come to] establish [the Jerusalem of] wood and stones but that he came to establish the heavenly Zion and the Spiritual Jerusalem, in that he spoke in terms of the faith for from that day on those who believe in him are saved. This is foolishness. He destroyed the visible but you say that he established the invisible! Thus you understand [this] in accord with your belief in him. *And of Zion it shall be said, This man and that man were born there* refers to the terrestrial Jerusalem. It is clear that the (names of) the countries he mentioned previously, *Rahab and Babylon ... Philistia and Tyre, with Ethiopia* are all on earth. Why do you not subject your belief to reason in an honest manner. [Scripture] speaks to a mature man, one who knows how to scrutinize his faith so that he will not err. This is the main thing.

[79] Cf. comm. of Naḥmanides, Lev. 26:16; Naḥmanides, *Letter upon Arrival in Jerusalem,* ed. Yaari, *Mase'ot Ereẓ Yisra'el,* p. 76.

Moreover, you believe other things unvindicated by reason even though Scripture rejects them, such as the belief that the dead perform miracles and wonders and that they pray to God *on behalf of the living (to the dead)* (Isa. 8:19). See that Scripture held liable [33a] those who consult the dead on behalf of the living: *Should not a people consult their God? [Should they consult] the dead on behalf of the living?* Scripture says further, *The dead do not praise God, nor do any who go down in silence* (Ps. 115:17). There is no evidence either that the first prophets, Abraham, Isaac, and Jacob, Moses and [all the other] prophets worked miracles after their death.

The *min* said: Do you not see that it is customary for people to appeal to princes, nobles, and officials to speak to the king on their behalf? So do these dead plead for people.

The *ma'amin* said: A human being may convince a prince to speak on his behalf. The prince will go to the king and say, "My lord, if he has done wrong he will not continue to do you wrong, but from this day onwards, he will be your faithful servant. Forgive then his wrongdoing and forget his crimes." Now the king does not know [what is in] the heart[s] of men and so he believes the words of the princes. If his repentance is genuine, there is no need for saints to intercede for the sinner. The Creator has already promised him who is sincere in repentance that He will accept him. If however he lies deceitfully and feigns repentance, what good is the prayer of the dead or the living if they pray for him or ask mercy. If it becomes clear to Him that his repentance is false and deceitful, the Creator will not listen to all the dead saints, all who inhabit the earth, and all the heavenly angels [together]. If his repentance is genuine, he will need no other aid, for his repentance will be his aid.[80]

[80] Christian seeking of the intercession of saints was attacked throughout the middle ages. See Blumenkranz, *TZ* IV (1948), 145f.; Rosenthal, *Meḥqarim,* I, 450.

Now, my beloved friend,[81] I have explained to you some questions and answers with which to refute those who believe in a man who is no god. May God keep you, my son and disciple. God illumine your eyes with His Torah. May He teach you and show the path which you must follow. May He keep you from the way of fools and those who err in their belief.

Up to this point, I have outlined for you some [33b] of the questions which are generally asked by gentiles and I have explained the replies of the *min* who proves his faith from our Torah. If he asks you a question other than those questions about which I have advised you, then [you must] study over and over again those questions discussed explicitly in this book. Using them as a model, you will be able to answer others.

My intention now is to explain to you all the passages in which there are consolations or prognostications for Israel. I shall show you the manner in which they usually interpret the consolations. When you find a consolation for Israel, they say, "We are the sons of Jacob." When they find a consolation for Judah, they say to you....[82]

THE "ADDITIONS" TO THE *BOOK OF THE COVENANT*

A reply to the deniers: *Will you still say, "I am a god," in the presence of those who slay you, though you are but a man and no god, in the hands of those who wound you.* (Ez. 28:9) This is an irrefutable reply.[82a]

[81] The author here addresses his student.

[82] The original dialogue breaks off with the discussion of "verus Israel". Cf. *JbR,* p. 53; Isaac Abravanel, *Yeshu'ot Meshiḥo,* (Königsburg, 1860), p. 58b; *HUCA* XXXVIII (1967), 222f.

[82a] Cf. *Yosef ha-Meqanne,* ed. Rosenthal, p. 72.

The *min* asked further: Why do you not believe that Jesus entered the womb of Mary to become incarnate, when it is written, *the sons of God saw how beautiful the daughters of man were.* (Gen. 6:2)

The reply of the *ma'amin:* Our teacher Moses, of blessed memory, informed us that it is impossible that the spirit of the Creator become incarnate, as it is said, *My spirit will not abide in man for ever in that he is flesh* (Gen. 6:3), i.e. "My spirit will never be in man because he is flesh" and also because the days of man are only one hundred and twenty years. Yet if you say that [his refusal to abide in man applies only to a man *('adam)* and] not to a woman, we have found *'adam* applied to a woman: *with the beauty of* 'adam *to dwell in a house* (Isa. 44:13).[83]

The *min* asked further: Why did they crucify Jesus?

The sage, R. Joseph Kara,[84] of blessed memory, replied: Because of the "generation of division" that built the Tower, God came down to see the Tower and said: "Why do you wish to ascend to heaven? I have given you the earth for [your] domain". He consequently threw down the Tower and slew them. Thus, when Jesus came and said he was God, they said "[You] are walking on our earth! Are not the heavens yours? For David said, *The heavens are the Lord's heavens* (Ps. 115:16)." They thereupon raised him on high lifting him up to the heavens in the thought that he would return to his own dominion. [In this way] was he hanged.[85]

[83] It is possible that there is an allusion here to the bodily assumption of Mary which began to gain currency in this period. See M. Jugie, *La Mort et l'Assumption de la Sainte Vierge* (Vatican, 1944). On *'adam* as meaning woman, see *Yosef ha-Meqanne,* ed. Rosenthal, pp. 55f.

[84] See introduction, p. 18, n.45.

[85] See introduction, p. 26.

Further, [34a] why do you not believe in "the hanged one", for it is written, *your life shall hang* (Dt. 28:66)?[86]

[*The ma'amin*] said: In Scripture itself, Moses prohibited believing in him, when he said, *you shall not believe in your life* (Dt. 28:66).

The root of belief is implanted in the waters of reason and understanding, wisdom and true knowledge. *The precepts of the Lord are right* (Ps. 19:8). My lord, master, and teacher, the distinguished and eminent sage, my grandfather, R. Eliezer[87] the son of the noted R. Samuel, *may his soul dwell in goodness and his seed inherit the earth* (Ps. 25:13), remarked: The sure, concise arguments which reject the opinion of those who believe in a created God [invoke] the power of reason and a knowledge of the Torah, the Prophets, and Writings. Moses and his Torah are true and Jesus and his teaching are false. [One must] believe in the Lord God, the God of Israel, the living God Who is the life of the universe, from Whom comes the soul of all living. He has never changed nor will He ever change. No man has seen Him and lived. He is the God of gods Who caused His glory to dwell on Mount Sinai and Who gave us Torah and commandments through Moses, the servant of the Lord. This was made evident to all the nations (who today have denied the Lord) by performing miracles for the multitude. He split the sea for them and sank the Egyptians in it; He performed miracles in the wilderness to fulfill the covenant with the patriarchs. Because He loved our forefathers, He introduced them to His service and gave them the two tablets of stone through [Moses], the faithful messenger of His household. [They were] inscribed

[86] "Your life" is taken to refer to Jesus. Cf. Yair ben Shabbethai of Corregio *Ḥerev Pipiyot*, ed. J. Rosenthal (Jerusalem, 1968), p. 90.

[87] See introduction, p. 18, n.45.

on both sides[88] so that the Gentiles and all the nations which were to follow could not say that God had not completed His work, having left one side of the tablets empty so that He might write other laws and a new Torah. [The writing] was *engraved on the tablets* (Ex. 32:16) so that it could be erased and so that they could not say that their baptismal waters which were to come could erase the writing in the holy Torah of Moses. They were inscribed on both sides *in the same language* and in a *few words*[89] to teach with completeness, wisdom, and knowledge. One may not add to the Torah nor take anything away. We may add another reason as to why they were inscribed on both sides. The tablets and the fragments [of the first] tablets were placed in the ark.[90] Thus the inscription pointed to the heavens above and the earth beneath. On the two tablets of stone, inscribed [34b] by the finger of God, were the ten commandments. They heard the [first] two commandments, the first statement *I am* and *you shall have no* ... directly from God, that is to say, without an intermediary. They were worthy of hearing these two statements from the mouth of God because of the two noble words, *we will do and we will hear* (Ex. 24:7), by which they proclaimed [their desire] to perform the will of their Creator [and] to receive the Torah. Thus did our Rabbis say: "Once God has spoken, twice have we heard this.[91] That which the mouth cannot utter and the ear not hear! This teaches that both [commandments] were uttered simultaneously".[92] We can say too that because of the two words which they said, Moses wrote the ten commandments on two stones as a memorial rather than on one or three. As a memorial of this also there

[88] Palestinian Talmud, Sheqalim 6:1.
[89] Cf. Gen. 11:1.
[90] Palestinian Talmud, Sotah 8:3.
[91] Cf. Ps. 68:12.
[92] Cf. Mekhilta, Masekhta de-shirta, 8.

were two cherubs and two poles.[93] Now since our fathers have seen His greatness, glory, and power and have heard His voice from the midst of the fire, and since *He has not dealt thus with any other nation* (Ps. 147:20), we are not to charge God with wrong, nor to transgress His commandments, nor to exchange Him for another god. We have therefore been committed to His divinity and His unity over above any other commandment which God gave us through Moses our teacher, peace be upon him. Thus have we found many who have undergone martyrdom for the sake of "the sanctification of the Name" but who have not done so [in order to avoid transgressing the prohibition against] illicit sexual relationships and other transgressions. Indeed, in the days of the prophets, when they transgressed [the prohibitions] against illicit relations, they would practice idolatry, not out of love [for it], but so that the prophets would not reprove them for the other sins when they saw that they had denied God. Our Rabbis have discussed this in the eleventh chapter of tractate *Sanhedrin*.[94]

When God commanded *I* [*am the Lord*] *and* you *shall have no* [*other gods*], He appended the prohibition against making a sculptured image, or any likeness of what is in the heavens above or the earth below and against bowing down to them or serving them.[95] [This is prohibited] even [if done with the intent of] honoring heaven, even though one does not

[93] Ex. 37:4, 5; 7.

[94] The reference would appear to be to the story concerning David who pretended to worship idols for an ulterior motive. See Babylonian Talmud, Sanhedrin 107a.

[95] Christian polemical literature frequently responds to Jewish accusations of idolatry in connection with images. See Agobard, *De superst. iud.* 10, *PL* CIV, 88; *AJ*, pp. 162, 167, 174, 177, 272, 374, 379. Cf. *JbR*, p. 100; *Teshuvot ha-Minim* in Rosenthal, *Meḥqarim*, I, 37; Eliyahu Hayyim of Genezzano, *Disp.* in Rosenthal, *Meḥqarim* I, 443; Blumenkranz, *TZ* IV (1948), 146. On the Jews as a catalyst in the iconoclast controversies, see B. Blumenkranz, *Juifs et Chrétiens dans le Monde Occidental* (Paris, 1960), pp. 288ff. See also Baron, *Soc. and Rel. Hist.*, V, 347, n. 56.

accept [the idol itself] as a god nor believe in it. [We may conclude this since] He has already stated the prohibition concerning one who believes in an image and accepts it as a god in the statement *You shall have no other gods* [35a] *beside Me.* Our master Moses, on whom be peace, gave a reason for this: *Since you saw no shape [when the Lord your God spoke to you at Horeb of the fire, do not ... make for yourselves a sculptured image....]* (Deut. 4:15). Therefore, the Christians who make images and bow down before them are transgressors, for they too were commanded against idolatry which is one of the seven commandments given to the sons of Noah.[96] David cursed [such as] these: *They who make them will be like them* (Ps. 115:8, 135:18). Now since the Creator of all prohibited us from worshipping other gods and from making images, even [if consecrated] to Him, we most certainly must not accept as a god one who was born of woman and who ate, drank and performed other bodily functions for thirty years and then died.

Now they have a claim according to which they say that he came to assume substance and form, death and suffering to atone for the sin of Adam and Eve by which they transgressed [God's] commandment. Thus they would no longer be under His curse, [uttered] when He warned them of the tree of knowledge, *as soon as you eat of it, you shall be doomed to die* (Gen. 2:18). They say that He meant a double death – the body in this world and the soul in the world to come[97] – and they think that all the righteous who died before his coming underwent death and suffering and were condemned to Gehenna. On this account, he underwent death and suffering

[96] Babylonian Talmud, Sanhedrin 56a.

[97] The Hebrew reads *mot tamut* using two verbal forms for the root *mwt* = to die. The notion of the "*mors duplex*" is found in Ambrose, *Liber de Paradiso* I:43, ed. Cailleau et Guillon, p. 306. Cf. *Yosef ha-Meqanne,* ed. Rosenthal, p. 36.

to redeem them from the death of body and soul. To this there are many answers.[98]

The first answer, which is brief and rational: If Adam sinned, how did their god sin?

The second answer: If, as they say, it is true that he came to assume substance, form, and death in order to atone for the sin of Adam and Eve, why did those men and women who came after him undergo death and suffering? Was not the sin fully atoned by the death of Jesus, as they say? Why from that day on does man still eat bread by the sweat of his brow and woman still give birth in pain? From the day that Jesus their god appeared to this, not one item has been cancelled in the curse which God pronounced over [Adam and Eve] for the sin of the fruit of the tree.

The third answer: *The precepts of the Lord are true and altogether righteous* (Ps. 19:9) and [follow the principle of] measure for measure [35b] and like for like. Thus it is said: *Measure by measure, by exile you contended with them* (Isa. 27:8). Our Rabbis expounded: "Man is measured according to his own measure".[99] Thus did the Holy One, blessed be He, act toward the Egyptians when He drowned them [in punishment for Pharaoh's orders:] "*every boy ... you shall throw into the Nile*" (Ex. 1:22). There are many similar instances. If it is as they say, why was the man afflicted and not the woman? This is not measure for measure! She who had conceived their god who was to be born should have given birth to a male and a female. It would have been fitting for the woman to have undergone death and suffering moreso than for the man, since the woman initiated the transgression. The serpent caused her to seduce her husband and she gave him of the fruit of the tree. We have so found that the woman was

[98] See above, pp. 36ff.
[99] Babylonian Talmud, Sotah 8b.

more cursed than the man for she gives birth in pain, while the man does not procreate in pain and was not so cursed. It would appear then that there exists a contradiction in their theology over this and they are compelled to say that women have not been forgiven the sin of the woman Eve. Further, nothing can be proved from the use of two terms [from the root *mwt*] meaning "death", for Scripture speaks in ordinary language. There are many instances like this in the Torah.

The fourth answer: If it is as they say, why did they tarry almost four thousand years? Throughout this time, there had passed several generations more righteous and good than the generation he came to redeem. They themselves admit that our patriarchs, that our Master Moses, and that our prophets were all completely righteous and true prophets of the living God and eternal King. Now if their god is God, why did he let them suffer in Gehenna until he appeared and was born? He was a man in every respect for thirty-two years and underwent sentence of death without redeeming them throughout all that time according to their words.

The fifth answer concerns their statement that the souls of the righteous descended to Gehenna. Scripture proves their error for their fathers inherited falsehood. Concerning the death of Abraham, it states in the Torah that God said to him, *As for you,* [36a] *you shall go to your fathers in peace, you shall be buried at a ripe old age* (Gen. 15:15). If it is as they say, where is the peace and ripe old age told him by the Holy One, blessed be He, if, as according to them, he is to go down to Gehenna. It would appear then *that their right hand is a right hand of falsehood* (Ps. 144:8).

In reply to their saying that our exile has been protracted because we inflicted torments on their god, we shall say that their words are without substance, for God does not punish without forewarning. Thus with the sin of Adam and Eve, He warned [Adam] beforehand and said to him, *You shall not eat of the tree of knowledge of good and evil,* etc. (Gen. 2:17). Therefore, He punished them because they transgressed His commandment. In many places in the Torah, you will so find that God does not punish unless He has forewarned.[99a] If it is as they say, He should, with respect to belief in this man, have forewarned in the Torah of Moses our master that one should believe in him when he comes, grows, and is weaned, since, according to them, every reward in the universe is dependent on him.

We find the reason as to why our exile was to come about in the Torah. It was not because of this (the crucifixion). Rather were we to be scattered among the nations because of our having abandoned the Torah of our God and His commandments and statutes – for no other reason! Then He promised us that He would gather up our exiles from the four corners [of the earth] and that He would protect us in our exile, as it is written, *Yet, even then, when they are in the land of their enemies* [I will not reject them], etc. (Lev. 26:44).

They say further that our exile has been protracted because we inflicted torments on their god so that ever since we have not prospered, regressing instead of progressing. Tell them that it is they who say that Jesus descended to the world in order to suffer by his own free will in order to save the world from Satan. Before his coming, all souls walked in darkness and gloom – even the righteous such as Abraham. If he did not want to undergo these afflictions, nobody could have harmed him even if they had banded together. It was so written in the Gospels that once the Jews went to capture Jesus at nighttime. Jesus said, "Whom do you [36b] seek"?

[99a] Cf. e.g. Babylonian Talmud, Sanhedrin 56a.

They said, "We seek Jesus". Jesus answered and said, "I am Jesus". Immediately, they started back and fell like corpses and were unable to capture him".[100]

The gentiles say that the time had not yet come when he was to suffer. This proves that according to them he was afflicted when he wished it so. Accordingly, he descended to earth to die and save the world from the torment of hell. Why then did he punish the nation that dealt rightly with him,[101] since by his own free will he accepted death? Had the Jews not wanted to kill him, he would have put it into their hearts to do so, since he was God and it was so decreed from above by his father in heaven. He underwent death to save the world for in no other way could he have saved the world from the torment of hell. Only by his blood and his death, according to their notion, did he redeem the world from Satan's power. If so, he committed a grave injustice in punishing the nation that killed and afflicted him according to his own wishes. We can say too that the intention of the Jews was positive, since they heard from his own mouth that the salvation of the world was dependent upon his death. [They wished then] that the world be saved through them that they might have some merit in the world to come in this matter. Therefore, they killed him to save the world.

We can state too another irrefutable reply [based on what is] written in the Gospel. It is written in the Gospel that when they afflicted Jesus, Jesus cried out to his father and said, *My father, forgive this people for they know not what they do* [cf. Luke 23:34]. If it is so that the prayed for us to his father to

[100] As reported in *Toledot Yeshu* in J. Eisenstein, *Oẓar Wikkuḥim* (New York, 1928), 228f.

[101] The Hebrew may be read *meyashsherim* as here or *meyasserim* meaning "afflicted". On the question of actual guilt in the crucifixion, see H. H. Ben Sasson, "Yiḥud 'am yisra'el le-da'at bene ha-me'ah ha-shtem-'esreh", *Peraqim* II, (Jerusalem, 1971), pp. 29ff.

forgive us, either his prayer was sincere [or it was not]. If his prayer and supplication were sincere, his death and the sufferings he underwent are forgiven us. It is not right that we undergo any punishment for his death since he forgave us and prayed for us. If his prayer is not sincere and he said one thing with his mouth [37a] and another in his heart, then the rest of his words are insincere.

Further, how [could] he pray to his father that he might not die, saying *You are my father. If it is possible, take the cup of death from me. Let this be only in accord with your will* [cf. Matt. 26:39].[101a] Now if he prayed with respect to the [salvation of his] flesh, his prayer was not accepted, he was not to be considered a righteous man. Thus David said, *The eyes of the Lord are toward the righteous,* etc. (Ps. 34:16); *when they cry the Lord hears,* etc. *(ibid.,* v. 18); *Many are the afflictions of the righteous,* [*but the Lord delivers him out of them all*] *(ibid.* v. 20); *The eye of the Lord is on those who fear Him,* etc. (*ibid.,* 33:18); *to deliver their soul from death (ibid.,* v. 19); and many other verses beside these. Further, he prayed [for that which was against his father's will], for He sent him to undergo death and he asked not to die.

[Now] if he prayed with respect to [his] divinity, the Divinity needs no help from others (Heaven forbid!) but is a help to others.

Further, he himself instructed, *Forgive this people for they know not what they do.* It follows than that it was not their intention to kill the son of God but that it was their intention to kill a human being, the son of a man and a woman. No sin is [to be imputed] to them because [all] things [are considered] with respect to the intention of the heart. Therefore, they are not justified in saying that by trying Jesus, our exile has been protracted for many years.

Let us return to the subject. We see today with our very eyes His many deeds of kindness and His great mercy in that He has not ceased to act in righteousness and truth with His people these twelve hundred years. Further, He preserved our exile [brought about] by our iniquities and did not abandon us or break His covenant with us. We, [on our part], did not forget His holy Torah. Even the women know the commandments and precepts and are expert in the subtleties of rabbinic tradition, such as the separation of *ḥallah*,[102] the lighting of the candles on the Sabbath, and the oil of the thigh muscle![103] We rely upon them even in the matter of porging meat which involves prohibition against blood and fat forbidden by the Torah.[104] (This is against the[105] opinion of certain of our sages who have ruled that one is not to rely upon them in something [directly] prohibited by the Torah. Their proof [is based] upon that which is said in [the Talmudic tractate] Ketubot[106]; viz. if we did not have the [explicit] statement in Scripture, [*When she becomes clean of her discharge,*] *she shall count off* [*seven days, and after that she shall be clean*] [Lev. 15:28], she would not be trusted [to count the days of her] ritual uncleanness because it involves a [direct] prohibition of the Torah. [As further proof, they cite] the first chapter of tractate Pesaḥim where it states that the Rabbis trust them concerning rabbinical enactments[107] and the Palestinian Talmud which states "women are lazy and search slowly".[108] They

[102] *JE* VI, 174f.
[103] Cf. Gen. 32:32.
[104] *JE* X, 132.
[105] It would appear that this passage is a later gloss.
[106] Babylonian Talmud, Ketubot 72a.
[107] Babylonian Talmud, Pesaḥim 4b.
[108] Palestinian Talmud, Pesaḥim 1:1.

explain [that this is so because] they do not know how to search properly. Yet all this is not of central importance since women are certainly [to be considered] reliable with respect to every prohibition which lies within their province – even a prohibition from the Torah.[109] The verse mentioned in Ketubot, *she shall count off,* is needed because without it she would not know how to proceed. Their proof from the statement in Pesaḥim does not amount to anything either. Nor is the Palestinian Talmud to be interpreted as they do. It means that because women are lazy, they are apprehensive lest they be suspected of not having searched properly and [consequently] search especially carefully. Let us return to our subject.)[105] During these more than twelve hundred years during which our exile has lasted, we have not forgotten the perfect Torah of our God [or] His commandments or statutes. They shall never again be forgotten by us or by our descendants, according to the text which says, *As for Me, this is My covenant with them, says the Lord: My spirit which is upon you* [*and My words which I have put in your mouth, shall not depart out of your mouth, or out of the mouth of your children, or out of the mouth of your children's children, says the Lord, from this time forth and forevermore* [Isa. 59:21]. It was only in the seventy years of the Babylonian exile that they forgot the entire Torah – even the keeping of the Sabbath – until Ezra the prophet came. He reproved them, [telling them] to repent, not to carry a burden from their houses on the Sabbath day, and to divorce their foreign women, the Hittite and Moabite women whom they took as wives.[110] They listened to him, repented, went up to Jerusalem, and built the great and holy House. Now behold the works of the Lord! In these more than twelve hundred years that

[109] This discussion, with a conclusion similar to that of the author, is found in R. Menaḥem ha-Meiri, *Bet ha-Beḥirah* on Pesaḥim (Tel Aviv, 1964), p. 7.
[110] Cf. Neh. 13:14ff.

our exile has lasted, we have not forgotten His holy Torah nor [have we ceased] to believe that He in His righteousness keeps the gracious covenant with our fathers and with us as He has promised us in the Torah, *Yet, even then, [when they are in the land of their enemies, I will not reject them]*, etc. (Lev. 26:44).

After the death of Moses the servant of the Lord, the former and latter prophets also wrote against believing in a god that underwent death. The first [was] Joshua who, when Israel was at the bank of the Jordan, said, *Tomorrow the Lord will do wonders for you* (Jos. 3:5) and promised them that they would cross the Jordan by foot as they did.[38a] Afterwards he said, *By this you shall know that the living God is among you* (*ibid*., v. 10) and used the phrase *living God* to exclude [the possibility of a dead] god who has no power to work wonders. It is written in many places in the other prophets, *As the Lord of hosts lives* (I Kings 18:15), that is to say "He lives forever." In the book of Hosea, who is among the latter prophets, it is written, *Yet the number of the people of Israel shall be like the sand of the sea,* etc. and then at the end, *it shall be said of them "Sons of the living God"* (Hos. 2:1). Elijah the prophet also alluded to us that our holy Torah, which is likened to fire as it is said *a fiery law unto them* (Dt. 33:2), is everlasting and no amount of water will be able to extinguish it. Rather it would remain forever. The proof is that after it was written that the fire of God had consumed the dust, the wood, and the stones, why did he have to write the conclusion *and licked up the water that was in the trench.* (I Kings 18:38)? It is that he wanted to allude [to the fact] that the fire of our holy religion would consume the water which is the baptismal water of Christianity.[111] May the God who answered him with

[111] The account of Elijah's offering was interpreted Christologically by Christian exegetes. See *Glossa Ordinaria,* ed. Venice, 1603, II, col. 828

fire sustain the fire of our holy religion. May He quickly send one who will announce to us the coming of the redeemer to gather the dispersed of Israel. Amen. Selah. May it be [His] will and let us say Amen.

SELECT BIBLIOGRAPHY

BLUMENKRANZ, Bernard, *Juifs et Chrétiens dans le monde occidental, 430-1096,* Paris: Mouton, 1960.

BRAUDE, Morris, *Conscience on Trial,* New York: Exposition Press, 1962.

GRAYZEL, Solomon, *The Church and the Jews in the XIIIth Century,*[2] New York: Hermon Press, 1966.

MOORE, George Foote, "Christian Writers on Judaism", *Harvard Theological Review* XIV (1921), 197-254.

RANKIN, Oliver S., *Jewish Religious Polemics of Earlier and Later Centuries,* Edinburgh: University Press, 1956.

SIMON, Marcel, *Verus Israel,* Paris: E. de Boccard, 1964.

SYNAN, Edward A., *The Popes and the Jews in the Middle Ages,* New York: The Macmillan Company, 1965.

TALMAGE, Frank, "R. David Kimḥi as Polemicist", *Hebrew Union College Annual* XXXVIII (1967), 213-35.

WILLIAMS, Arthur Lukyn, *Adversus Judaeos,* Cambridge: University Press, 1935.

INDEX

INDEX OF SCRIPTURAL PASSAGES

(The numbering is that of the masoretic text. Where the Vulgate numeration differs, it appears in parentheses.)